the complete guide to

simple swimming

From terrified to terrific

Everything you need to know from first entering the
water, to performing the four basic swimming strokes

mark young

A Catalogue record for this book is available from the British Library

ISBN 978-0-9570031-5-6

Published by: Educate & Learn Publishing, Hertfordshire, UK

E&L   enquiries@educateandlearnpublishing.com

Graphics by Mark Young, courtesy of Poser V6.0

Design and typeset by Mark Young and Baines Design, Cuffley, UK

For Viki, Francesca & Carys

contents

contents

chapter 1

why swim?

It's a well known fact, and years of research back it up, that swimming provides many physical, social and psychological benefits. They include increased cardiovascular fitness , improved strength and flexibility, enhanced muscular stamina and balance, a stronger heart

with increased cardiovascular endurance, and positive changes in body shape and body composition. Apart from this, swimming also works as a fast and effective remedy for healing muscles, due to its zero impact and high repetitive nature.

One of the most important reasons for learning to swim has to be safety. Swimming pools and open water areas such as lakes and rivers are an attractive source of fun and entertainment and as a result quite often the dangers of water can be overlooked.

Fun

The importance for children to learn how to swim cannot be underestimated, and respect for the water should be taught as early as possible. As children grow and develop, their strength and therefore ability to move around in the water, with or without floatation aids, also increases. This in turn opens up a whole world of fun and enjoyment. This brings us to the next most important reason to learn to swim: fun.

Most of us, particularly children, swim for fun. With fun comes health and fitness in the form of exercise and activity, and most swimming pools and leisure facilities are in local areas and are relatively inexpensive.

It is important to note, that children should always be supervised around water, regardless of their swimming ability. The most competent of swimmers can get into trouble at any time and in any water environment. Nobody is drown-proof!

Swimming exercise also helps to reduce body fat and can relieve your mind from stress and tension, keeping you in perfect shape, physically as well as mentally.

The benefits of swimming are huge for individuals who are obese, or individuals suffering from orthopaedic conditions such as lower back problems. This activity offers some aerobic benefits and unlike other weight training programs, swimming does not put strain on weight bearing joints, as it is a zero impact activity.

Research indicates that pregnant women benefit the most from swimming. It makes their abdominal muscles strong, which are most essential when carrying a baby. In addition, it strengthens the back and the muscles that help post-mastectomy women carry their weight more easily. According to experts, exercising in water can considerably reduce joint stiffness, high blood pressure, and discomfort, which is often associated with pregnancy.

rehabilitation

Swimming is a great means of injury rehabilitation and is also a very effective way of recovering after surgery. Muscles and joints need a gentle re-introduction to exercise as part of their rehabilitation process and swimming provides them with just that.

After a woman has undergone breast surgery, doctors often suggest it as part of the recovery process. This is considered to be an advantageous means of exercising all the major muscle groups.

It is advisable that you consult a physician before commencing a rehabilitation program. It is very important to talk to experts as they can confirm which swimming strokes are moderate and which can be strenuous.

There is also a low risk for swimming injuries because there's no stress on your body due to the extremely low levels of impact on the joints and bones. As a safe daily workout routine, swimming is perfect because you can rigorously work out with a reduced chance of injury. Many athletes supplement their training with swimming as it provides effective cardiovascular workouts that make significant increases in cardiovascular endurance.

As your cardiovascular fitness increases and you are able to swim longer distances, your resting heart rate and respiratory rate will be reduced, making blood flow to the heart and lungs more efficient. Swimming is also a very effective form of calorie burning and therefore weight loss. On average, a swimmer can burn as many calories in an hour as a runner who runs six miles in one hour. Simply put, some call swimming the perfect form of exercise. Swimming fitness tones your upper and lower body simultaneously because you're using almost all of your major muscle groups, and therefore provides all-over body toning.

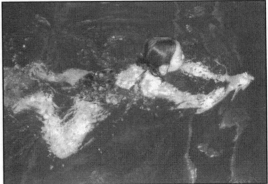

Swimming is an important life skill that teaches us water safety as well as has many other benefits. Being able to swim gives us the opportunity to take part in fun, enjoyable water exercise and maintain cardiovascular health. Understanding water conditions is an essential part of participating in many outdoor activities. Most people will learn to swim at a swimming pool, which is the safest environment in which to learn. It can also be a calm and relaxing place to learn how to overcome the fear of water.

chapter 2

swimming science

Understanding some of the key scientific principles of swimming will provide a greater understanding of how the human body behaves in water. It will also give a greater insight into how and why strokes are swum in the way that they are.

buoyancy

It is important to understand buoyancy and relative density when learning how to swim. A basic understanding of this is a crucial element of overcoming a fear of water.

Floating is a characteristic of the human body. Some of us have good buoyancy while others do not. It's all down to our relative density. In other words, how dense our body structure is, compared to the density of the water we are attempting to float in. Let us put some actual figures to this:

Freshwater has a density of **1g/cm^3**
Saltwater has a density of **1.024g/cm^3**, therefore having a higher density
The average male has a density of **0.98g/cm^3** and the average female **0.97g/cm^3**.

We can deduce therefore that most human beings will float to a certain degree, with a small amount of the body staying above the water surface.

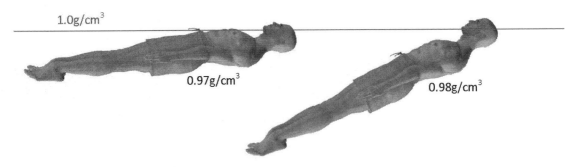

Females float better than males and both males and females float better in saltwater than in freshwater. Very few adults can float horizontally in the water, yet most children can hold a star float in the horizontal position.

It must be noted that a person's weight has little to do with their density. Muscle is denser and therefore heavier than fat, making fatter people better floaters. Other factors that effect floatation are:
- The volume of air in the lungs
- An individual's muscle to fat ratio
- The shape of the individual and therefore the location of their centre of gravity

Propulsion

Swimmers have to provide movement in the water in order to propel themselves through it. Types of movement we use most commonly are paddling, sculling and kicking.

Paddling is likened to oars on a boat. A large flat surface area pulled in one direction causes another object to move in the opposite direction. In the case of the human body, we pull or push with our hands and arms, causing us to move backwards or forwards in the water accordingly.

Sculling takes the form of a curved shape in the water made by the hands as they move to find still, undisturbed water. Water that is not moving provides more propulsion than water that has already been moved. All of the swimming strokes require some kind of sculling action. Sculling is the most efficient way of moving our hands and arms through the water.

Kicking the water with the legs is the least efficient way of moving through the water as it can require a rapid movement that can very quickly become tiring. It can be argued that kicking, be it in an up and down motion or a curved motion as in breaststroke, is another form of paddling or sculling. This is true, but kicking is often the first means of propulsion in the water that children discover and therefore can be classed as a separate form of propulsion.

Resistance

As the body moves through the water, it is met by resistance coming from the water itself. If this resistance is to be easily overcome, the body moving through the water has to be as streamlined as possible. There are three main types of resistance a swimmer will encounter in the water:

Profile resistance – this is the resistance met head on by the swimmer. As the swimmer moves forward through the water, the profile resistance is pushing him/her back. If profile resistance is to be minimised, the body has to be made as narrow and thin as possible.

Viscous drag – as a swimmer moves through the water, friction slows him/her down by creating a drag force. As water comes into contact with the skin, forward motion is compromised by the dragging force backwards. Excess body hair and baggy swimming shorts cause large increases in viscous drag.

Eddy currents – these are caused by an object moving through the water, causing the surrounding water to move and create turbulences. For example, if you place a floating object behind you as you swim, the object will follow you in the eddy current your swimming has created. Eddy currents are generally reduced when profile resistance is improved.

"The water is your friend...you don't have to fight with water, just share the same spirit as the water, and it will help you move".

Alexandr Popov - Olympic Gold Medallist

chapter 3

swimming aids

swimming aids

There is a wide range of swimming equipment available to help anyone learn to swim or improve their swimming strokes. All buoyancy and floatation aids can be used by non-swimmers to gain confidence and by competent swimmers to help improve various aspects of their strokes.

Artificial aids should be used as a form of enhancing confidence in the non swimmer when learning how to swim. The main purpose of artificial aids if you are a non-swimmers is to allow you to learn how to propel yourself through the water as soon as you have the confidence to do so.

arm bands

Arm bands, are probably the most commonly used swimming equipment in the pool and are best used for non-swimmers. Arm bands are very cheap and very durable floatation aids that are ideal for assisting young children in the early stages of learning to swim.

Advantages:

o Develop early confidence

o Buoyancy can be reduced by gradual deflation as the non-swimmer becomes stronger and more confident

o Co-ordination can be enhanced and improved as arms and legs can be used independently

arm bands

o A larger number of swimmers can be safely supervised

Disadvantages:

o Swimmers can become dependant on armbands and find it difficult to progress

o They can be restrictive and may hinder arm movement, especially in smaller children

o May not provide enough buoyancy if used by adults

A safety ring is a cheap and durable item of swimming equipment that is ideal for the non-swimmer. It is used mainly by children as a way of enhancing their confidence the water. The aid is worn around the body of the child and like armbands, it can restrict arm movements. It does however allow full movement and freedom of the legs.

They can be used in addition to arm bands, and in some cases with very small children the combination of armbands and safety ring is essential to prevent slipping through the ring.

As the child gains confidence, the ring should be discarded before the armbands, not vice-versa.

Advantages:

o   Allow the child's' face to be kept clear of the water

safety ring

o   Support the child at a higher level in the water

Disadvantages:

o   Can be insecure and some children can slip through

o   Can hinder arm action

o   Promotes a vertical body position

Another popular item of swimming equipment is the buoyancy suit. Suitable mainly for children, they promote floatation and enhance confidence and learning in the water. They are not as effective for complete non-swimmers as they do not keep the face out of the water in the same way that armbands do.

A floatation suit can promote a horizontal position in the water which is favourable for children that are comfortable with putting their face into the water. It can however be a hazard for children that do not have the strength in their arms or upper body to right themselves from a horizontal position.

buoyancy suit

Buoyancy suit continued:

Advantages:

o Can give a high level of support

o Allows unrestricted movement of the arms

o Can promote a horizontal position for the confident non-swimmer

o Allow the face to be kept clear of the water

Disadvantages:

o Pupils may find it difficult to regain the standing position

o Pupil may be tipped forward too far

float

A float is by far the most popular item of swimming equipment used in swimming due to their versatility and adaptability. They are suitable for non-swimmers right up to advanced swimmers, and can be used by both adults and children. Floats come in different sizes

depending on the needs of the swimmer and the size can often affect the level of buoyancy.

Two can be used by placing them one under each arm, giving added balance to the nervous or weak non-swimmer. One can be used to isolate and enhance strength in a particular aspect of the stroke.

Advantages:

o Very versatile and can be used in addition to other aids

o Can be used instead of other types of aid, therefore encouraging progression

o Can help gain leg or arm strength when used individually

Disadvantages:

o Requires a certain degree of strength in the leg kick

o One arm cannot be used

float

The noodle, or woggle as they are sometimes known, is an item of swimming equipment in the form of a polythene foam cylinder approximately 3 inches in diameter and 58 inches long.

The main advantage is that it provides a high level of support whilst as the same time allowing the swimmer movement of their arms and legs. The swimmer is able to learn and experience propulsion through the water from both the arms and the legs.

The noodle is very versatile and as it is not a fixed aid, it can be used and removed with ease. It can also add a sense of fun to swimming as it can be tucked under the arms on the front and the back as well as placed between the legs and used as a 'sea horse'.

Advantages

o Provides a high level of support

o Can be used by adults and children

o Easily used and removed

o Allows freedom of movement

Swim noodle

Disadvantages

o Limited use for advanced swimmers

o Nervous swimmers can 'clamp' it between their body and their arms, restricting their arm action

A pull buoy is a figure-eight shaped piece of swimming equipment made from solid foam and used mainly in swimming workouts. It is placed between the legs in the crotch area to provide support to the body without kicking the legs. This allows the swimmer to focus on arm technique.

Pull buoys are usually used by more advanced swimmers for training, as they are not suitable for non-swimmers as a buoyancy aid. They are designed to restrict the use of the swimmer's lower body, causing a greater intensity on the arms and upper body.

They are widely used by swimmers to provide resistance and isolate the arm action of a given stroke. They help to strengthen the upper body and arms by eliminating the kick propulsion, while keeping body position correct in the water.

Advantages:

o   Provide good isolation of the upper body

o   Ideal for work-outs and training

pull buoy

Disadvantages:

o   Not suitable for non-swimmers

SwimFin is the newest design of swimming equipment to the market and is revolutionising the way swimming is taught and learnt.

The Fin is secured comfortably to the back of the swimmer and it works with their natural buoyancy to help achieve the correct body position gradually over time. For example, it helps to provide support for the beginner, whose body position will be almost vertical. Over time as the swimmer become more confident, the Fin assists and aids a more natural, horizontal position. When a complete horizontal position is achieved, the Fin's assistance is virtually eliminated as it is above the water surface.

The overall swimming experience is enhanced by the fact that arms and legs are completely free to move and explore the water.

Advantages:

o Works with the swimmers natural buoyancy

o Encourages correct body position

o Allows completely free movement of arms and legs

o Can be used in conjunction with other swimming aids

o Enhances and builds confidence by encouraging freedom of movement

SwimFin

Disadvantages:

o A child can become dependent, so limited use is preferable

o Not suitable for very small children

All the swimming aids described here are mainly used to assist non-swimmers by keeping them afloat. Some can be used as swim training equipment by isolating certain parts of the swimming stroke so the swimmer can focus and train those weaker areas.

Swimmers and teachers should fully understand the purpose of any given artificial aid before administering its use. The use of the aid must be appropriate to the needs of the swimmer or non-swimmer and the teacher must be familiar with how to use it.

"I wouldn't say anything is impossible. I think that everything is possible as long as you put your mind to it and put the work and time into it".

Michael Phelps

chapter 4

the non-swimmer: essential basics

the non-swimmer: essential basics

Non-swimmers with the desire to learn how to swim arrive on the poolside in all different shapes, sizes and ages. Some will come with courage and confidence built in, many others will have a genuine fear of water and be scared witless! For some, arriving on the poolside will be a major achievement in itself.

entry

When learning how to swim, entering the swimming pool can be hugely daunting or very exciting for the non swimmer. Either way, it must be done in a safe and appropriate way.

The following methods of safe entry into the pool can be used accordingly:

Stepping in Using the Poolside Steps.

This is the best entry for the nervous non-swimmer.

You should enter by holding on to the rails with both hands and stepping down one step at a time. This is a safe and gradual entry that allows you to take your time.

The Sitting Swivel Entry

This entry works best on deck-level swimming pools, i.e. pools where the water is level with the poolside.

From a sitting position, with legs in the water…..

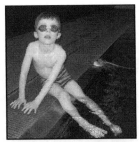
place both hands to one side….

and then turn your back to the water.

Then lower yourself gradually into the water, keeping hold of the poolside at all times.

Jumping Entry

Before using a jumping entry, you should consider the depth of the water compared to your own height. You should start with toes over the edge of the poolside, jump away from the poolside and bend your knees on landing.

This entry is best for more confident non-swimmers and should always be into water of a depth you are able to stand in. Buoyancy aids should always be worn by non-swimmers when performing this pool entry. If buoyancy aids are not being worn then the non-swimmer should jump towards a waiting assistant in the water.

submersion

When learning how to swim, the ability to submerge the face is arguably one of the most important stages when learning to swim, particularly when overcoming a fear of water. Some beginners arrive with this ability built in and only need to be taught how to breathe whilst swimming. For others it will be one of the most terrifying tasks you face. It goes without saying, the 'softly softly' approach is needed here. One stage at a time and only when you are happy and confident do you proceed to the next stage.

Stage 1: Getting the face wet

Remember, getting the face wet and being splashed in the face are two completely different concepts, each having different effects, and not always positive ones. Here are a few practices to work through:

Blowing bubbles on the water surface or blowing an object along as you swim. You can either blow gently 'like blowing through a straw' or blow with force 'like blowing out candles on a cake'.

Cupping water in your own hands and throwing it onto your face.

Throwing and catching a ball is an excellent distraction from the splashes of the water. If the ball is made to land just in front of you, this will result in a wet face without too much concern due to the distraction of catching the ball. The smallest of splashes from the softest of throws will be sufficient to have a positive effect.

Stage 2: Partially submerging the face

You first need to master the art of holding your breath by 'breathing in and holding it all in'.
Some will be able to do this easily, others will learn by trial and
error as you partially submerge your face and realise you are not
able to breath underwater!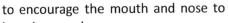

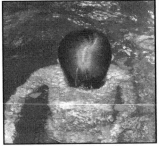

An object can then be placed just under the water surface,
shallow enough to see and reach for it, but deep enough for the
mouth to be submerged in order to reach it. Once confidence is
gained with this exercise, then the object can be lowered slightly
to encourage the mouth and nose to
be submerged.

These practices are best performed with an assistant in the water
holding the object for you. This may also help enhance your
confidence with someone in the water with you.

Stage 3: Total Submersion

Stage 2 naturally leads quickly onto stage 3 where the object is placed below the water
surface where you are encouraged to retrieve it by completely
submerging your head underwater. By this stage, breath holding
should be more accomplished and you should begin to relax more
as you submerge. Eventually learning how to swim becomes
easier.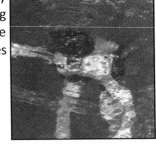

Progression from this stage is to incorporate face submerging,
either partially or completely, whilst swimming various strokes
and even retrieving objects from the pool floor during lengths or widths.

Theses 3 stages are crucial for overcoming a fear of water and gaining confidence in the
swimming pool. Those that have no fear of the water will work through the above 3 stages
with relative ease. For others it may take a few visits to the pool to get your confidence to
grow. Those with a fear of water may even wish to practice the first stage at home in the
bathroom.

regaining standing

Regaining a standing position from a face down (prone) position in the water is an essential movement to learn and is often overlooked when learning how to swim and overcoming the fear of water. Once you are able to execute this movement confidently, then your confidence will be enhanced. Knowing you are able to stand up from a floating or moving position will spur you on to greater things.

For complete beginners, an ideal starting point is from holding the poolside or floats held under each arm. As confidence grows, you can attempt standing without assistance, which requires a greater use of the arms and hands. This can also be progressed to a moving exercise, moving first towards and then away from the poolside.

Movement should be relaxed and smooth, knees are drawn forward as the arms simultaneously pull downward and backwards as the head lifts and faces forward.

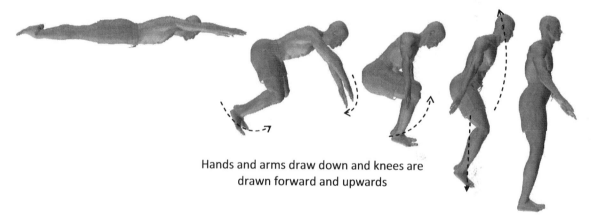

Hands and arms draw down and knees are drawn forward and upwards

Hands pull backwards as the head lifts and the feet are placed on the pool floor

Key Focus Points
o Pull down and back with both arms
o Bend your knees forwards as if to sit
o Lift your head upwards
o Place your feet on the pool floor

Common Faults
o The movement is rushed and not relaxed
o Failure to bend the knees
o Arching the back
o Failure to pull down and back with the hands

regaining standing

Regaining a standing position from a supine (face up) position in the water is another confidence building movement, essential to learning how to swim and overcoming the fear of water. The action is the opposite of the movement required for standing from a prone position.

For complete beginners, the best place to start is holding the floats or with a woggle held under the arms. As confidence grows you can attempt standing without assistance, which requires a greater use of the arms and hands. This can also be progressed to a moving exercise.

The movement should be relaxed and smooth as the knees are drawn towards the chest. The arms pull upwards and forwards and the head should lift and face forward as the feet are placed on the pool floor.

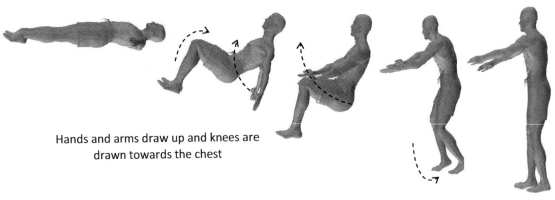

Hands and arms draw up and knees are
drawn towards the chest

Hands pull upwards as the head lifts and the feet are
placed on the pool floor

Key Points
o Pull both arms upwards to the surface
o Bend your knees forwards as if to sit
o Lift your head upwards
o Place your feet on the pool floor

Common Faults
o Movement is rushed and not relaxed
o Failure to bend the knees
o Arching the back
o Failure to pull up with both arms

chapter 5

front crawl

front crawl

Front crawl is the fastest, most efficient stroke of them all. This is largely down to the streamlined body position and continuous propulsion from the arms and legs.

The alternating action of the arms and legs is relatively easy on the joints and the stroke as a whole develops aerobic capacity faster than any other stroke. In competitive terms it is usually referred to as Freestyle.

The constant alternating arm action generates almost all of the propulsion and is the most efficient arm action of all strokes. The leg action promotes a horizontal, streamlined body position and balances the, arm action but provides little propulsion.

Freestyle breathing technique requires the head to be turned so that the mouth clears the water but causes minimal upset to the balance of the body from its normal streamlined position.

The timing and coordination of front crawl arms and legs occurs most commonly with six leg kicks to one arm cycle. However, stroke timing can vary, with a four beat cycle and even a two beat cycle, which is most commonly used in long distance swims and endurance events.

body position

The overall body position for this swimming stroke is streamlined and as flat as possible at the water surface, and the head in-line with the body.

The waterline is around the natural hairline with eyes looking forward and down.

If the position of the head is raised it will cause the position of the hips and legs to lower which in turn will increase frontal resistance.

If the head position is too low it will cause the legs to raise and the kick to lose its efficiency.

Shoulders remain at the surface and roll with the arm action. Hips also roll with the stroke technique, close to the water surface and the legs remain in line with the body.

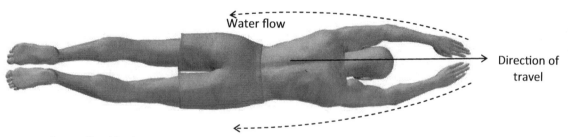

Streamlined body position minimises drag, allowing efficient movement through the water

legs

The leg kick for front crawl should originate from the hip and both legs should kick with equal force.

Legs kick in an up and down alternating action, with the propulsive phase coming from the down kick. There should be a slight bend in the knee due to the water pressure, in order to produce the propulsion required on the down kick.

The downward kick begins at the hip and uses the thigh muscles to straighten the leg at the knee, ending with the foot extended to allow it's surface area to bear upon the water. As the leg moves upwards, the sole of the foot and the back of the leg press upwards and backwards against the water.

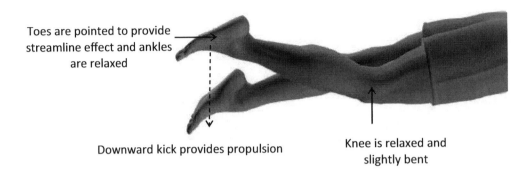

Toes are pointed to provide streamline effect and ankles are relaxed

Downward kick provides propulsion

Knee is relaxed and slightly bent

The upward kick slows and stops as the leg nears and minimally breaks the water surface. Ankles are relaxed and toes pointed to give an in-toeing effect when kicking and leg kick depth should be within the overall depth of the body.

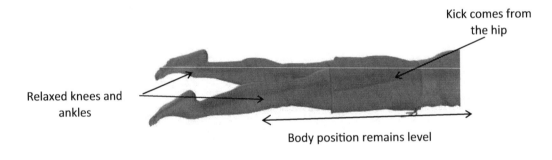

Kick comes from the hip

Relaxed knees and ankles

Body position remains level

arms

The continuous alternating arm action provides the majority of the power and propulsion of the entire swimming stroke.

- entry

Hand enters the water at a 45 degree angle, finger tips first, thumb side down. Hand entry should be between shoulder and head line with a slight elbow bend.

- catch

The hand reaches forward under the water without over stretching. Arm fully extends just under the water surface.

- propulsive Phase

Hand sweeps through the water downward, inwards and then upwards. Elbow is high at the end of the down sweep and remains high throughout the in-sweep. Hand pulls through towards the thigh and upwards to the water surface.

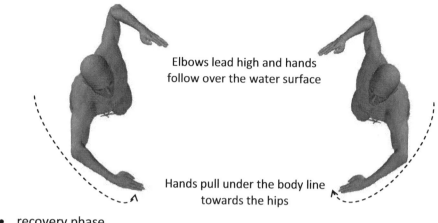

Elbows lead high and hands follow over the water surface

Hands pull under the body line towards the hips

- recovery phase

Elbow bends to exit the water first. Hand and fingers fully exit the water and follow a straight line along the body line over the water surface. Elbow is bent and high and the arm is fully relaxed.

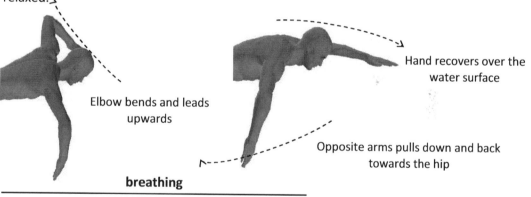

Elbow bends and leads upwards

Hand recovers over the water surface

Opposite arms pulls down and back towards the hip

breathing

The head turns to the side on inhalation for freestyle breathing technique. The head begins to turn at the end of the upward arm sweep and turns enough for the mouth to clear the water and inhale. The head turns back into the water just as the arm recovers over and hand returns to the water. Breathing can be bilateral (alternate sides every one and a half stroke cycles) or unilateral (same side) depending of the stroke cycle and distance to be swum.

Breath IN as the arm pulls through and the head turns to the side

Types of Breathing

- Trickle

The breath is slowly exhaled through the mouth and nose into the water during the propulsive phase of the arm pull. The exhalation is controlled to allow inhalation to take place easily as the arm recovers.

- Explosive

The breath is held after inhalation during the propulsive arm phase and then released explosively, part in and part out of the water, as the head is turned to the side.

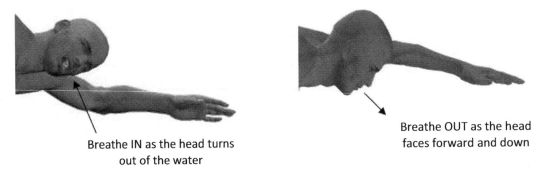

Breathe IN as the head turns
out of the water

Breathe OUT as the head
faces forward and down

timing

The timing and coordination for this swimming stroke usually occurs naturally.

Arms should provide a continuous power and propulsive alternating action whilst leg kicks also remain continuous and alternating.

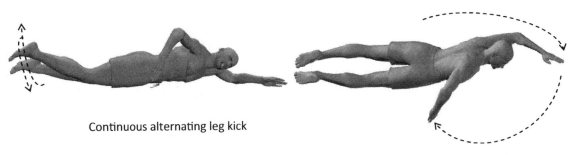

Continuous alternating leg kick

Continuous alternating arm action

However, there are a few variations.

- Six beat cycle – each legs kicks three down kicks per arm cycle. The cycle is normally taught to beginners and used for sprint swims.
- Four beat cycle – each leg kicks down twice for each arm pull.
- Two-beat cycle – each leg kicks one downbeat per arm cycle. This timing cycle is normally used by long distance swimmers, where the leg kick acts as a counter balance instead of a source of propulsion. This is not recommended for beginners.

full stroke overview

Level body position

Continuous alternating leg kick

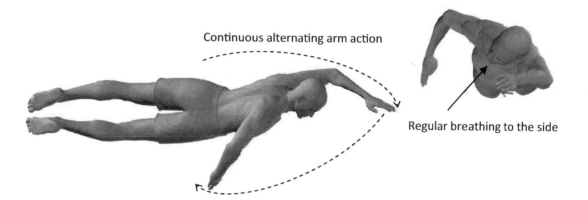

Continuous alternating arm action

Regular breathing to the side

"Enjoy swimming for swimming's sake. We have to spend far too much time in the water to not enjoy the process challenging yourself of moving through the water".

Jeff Rouse - Multiple Olympic Gold Medallist and swimming World Record setter

chapter 6

backstroke

This is the most efficient stroke swum on the back and is the third fastest of all swimming strokes. The majority of the power is produced by the alternating arm technique and its horizontal streamlined body position gives it its efficiency. Therefore this is the preferred stroke in competitive races swum on the back.

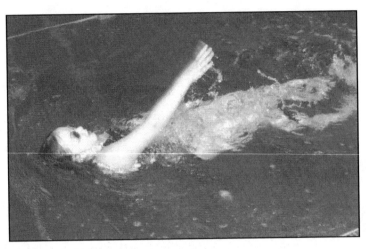

The nature of floating on the back, face up (supine) can be a calming and relaxing feeling. Also the face is clear of the water, allowing easy breathing and little water splashes onto the face. On the other hand it can be counter productive at first, as it can give a feeling of disorientation and unease, as the person is facing upwards and therefore unaware of their surroundings. The supine body position is flat and horizontal, with ears slightly below the water surface.

The legs kick in an alternating action, continuously up and down to help balance the action of the arms. This stroke has two different arm actions: the which is the most efficient, and the straight arm pull, which is the easiest to learn. Therefore the straight arm pull is best for beginners.

Breathing should be in time with recovery of each arm, breathing in with one arm recovery and out with the other. Ideally there should be 6 leg kicks to one arm cycle. This stroke timing may vary according to the swimmer's level of coordination.

The supine body position for this stroke is flat and horizontal, with ears slightly below the water surface.

Good floaters will find this position relaxing and relatively easy, whereas poor floaters will find it difficult to achieve a comfortable head position.

Body position remains horizontal and relaxed

The head remains still throughout the stroke with the eyes looking slightly down the body at a point the swimmer is swimming away from.

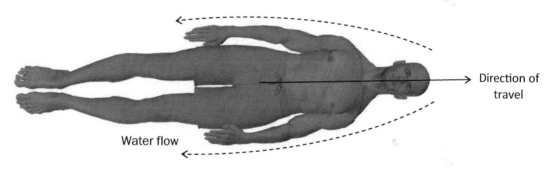

Direction of travel

Water flow

The head position is important because a raised head makes it more difficult to keep the hips raised in the correct position which leads to a sitting type position in the water.

The hips and shoulders remain at or near the water surface but roll with the stroke. The legs and feet should be extended and remain together to maximise efficiency, with knees remaining below the water surface.

legs

During this stroke the legs kick in an alternating action, continuously up and down to help balance the action of the arms.

Legs should be stretched out with toes pointed (plantar flexed) and ankles should be relaxed and loose with toes pointing slightly inwards.

The amount of propulsion generated from the kick will depend on the size of the feet, ankle mobility and strength of the legs.

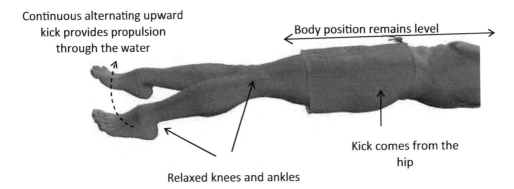

Continuous alternating upward kick provides propulsion through the water

Body position remains level

Kick comes from the hip

Relaxed knees and ankles

The knee should bend slightly and then straighten as the leg kicks upwards. Toes should kick to create a small splash but not break the water surface.

During specific leg practices the legs kick in a vertical plane. However, the arm action causes the body to roll making the legs kick part sideways, part vertical and partly to the other side.

---

arms

There are two possible arm actions for this stroke. The bent arm pull, which is more effective because it is faster and has greater propulsion, and the straight arm pull used in more recreational backstroke.

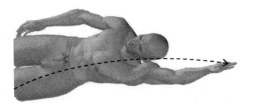

Arm rises upwards, little finger leading and arm brushing the ear

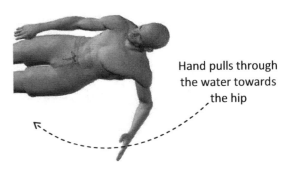

Hand pulls through the water towards the hip

- **straight arm pull**

entry
The arm should be straight and as inline with the shoulder as possible. Hand should be turned with palm facing outwards and little finger entering the water first.

propulsive phase
The arm sweeps through the water in a semi-circle, pulling with force just under the water surface, pulling to the outside of the thigh.

recovery

The thumb or the back of the hand should exit the water first. The shoulders roll again with the shoulder of the recovering arm rolling upwards. The arm rotates through 180 degrees over the shoulder. The palm is turned outwards during recovery to ensure that the hand enters the water little finger first.

- **bent arm pull**

As the arm pulls through to completion, the overall path should follow an 'S' shape.

entry

The entry is the same as the straight arm pull, with the little finger entering first, the palm facing out and the arm close to the shoulder line.

downward sweep

The palm should always face the direction of travel. The shoulders roll and the elbow bends slightly as the arm sweeps downwards and outwards.

upwards sweep

As the hand sweeps inline with the shoulder, the palm changes pitch to sweep upwards and inwards. The elbow should then bend to 9o degrees and point to the pool floor.

second downward sweep

The arm action then sweeps inwards towards the thigh and the palm faces downwards. The bent arm action is completed with the arm fully extended and the hand pushing downwards to counter balance the shoulder roll.

recovery

The thumb or the back of the hand should exit the water first. The shoulders roll again with the shoulder of the recovering arm rolling upwards. The arm rotates through 180 degrees over the shoulder. The palm is turned outwards during recovery to ensure that the hand enters the water little finger first.

---

breathing

Breathing during this stroke should be relaxed and easy, due to the supine body position and face being out of the water throughout the stroke. Most swimmers are neither aware of way in which they breathe, nor the pattern of breathing or point at which a breath is taken.

Breathing should be in time with recovery of each arm, breathing in with one arm recovery and out with the other. This encourages a breath to be taken at regular intervals.

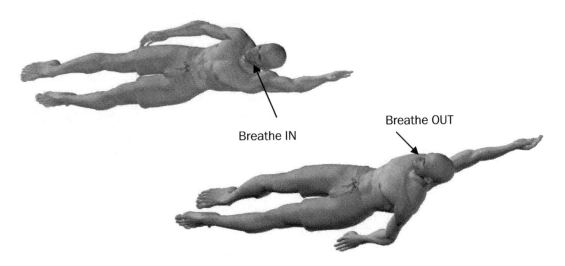

Breathe IN

Breathe OUT

A regular breathing pattern should be encouraged to prevent breath holding, particularly in beginners.

timing

The timing and coordination of the arms and legs develops with practice.

Ideally there should be 6 leg kicks to one arm cycle. The opposite leg kicks downwards at the beginning of each arm pull. This helps to balance the body. This may vary according to the swimmer's level of coordination.

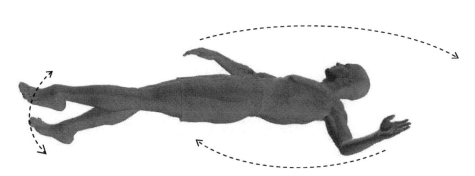

One arm exits the water as the other begins to pull and the leg kick remains continuous

Arm action should be continuous. i.e. when one arm enters and begins to pull, the other should begin its recovery phase.

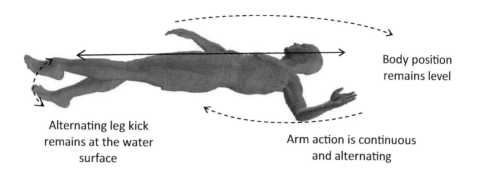

Body position
remains level

Alternating leg kick
remains at the water
surface

Arm action is continuous
and alternating

"You can't put a limit on anything. The more you dream, the farther you get".

Michael Phelps

chapter 7

breaststroke

breaststroke

This stroke is the oldest and slowest of the four swimming strokes. It is also the most inefficient of all strokes, which is what makes it the slowest. Propulsion from the arms and legs is a consecutive action that takes place under the water. A large frontal resistance area is created as the heels draw up towards the seat and the breathing technique inclines the,

body position also increasing resistance. These are the main reasons that make this stroke inefficient and slow.

This stroke is normally one of the first strokes to be taught, especially to adults, as the head and face is clear of the water, giving the swimmer a greater perception of their whereabouts and their buoyancy. There are variations in the overall technique, ranging from a slow recreational style to a more precise competitive style. Body position should be as flat and streamlined as possible with an inclination from the head to the feet so that the leg kick recovery takes place under the water.

The leg kick as a whole should be a simultaneous and flowing action, providing the majority of the propulsion.

The arm action should also be simultaneous and flowing and overall provides the smallest propulsive phase of the four strokes.

The stroke action gives a natural body lift which gives the ideal breathing point with each stroke and a streamlined body position during the timing sequence of the arm and leg action is essential to capitalise on the propulsive phases of the stroke.

body position

The body position should be inclined slightly downwards from the head to the feet.

The body should be as flat and streamlined as possible with an inclination from the head to the feet so that the leg kick recovery takes place under the water.

Head movement should be kept to a minimum and the shoulders should remain level throughout the stroke.

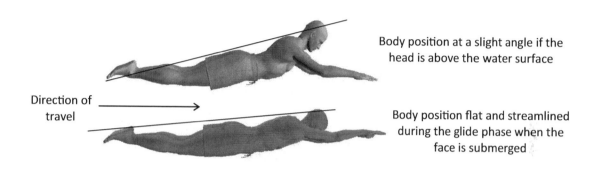

Body position at a slight angle if the head is above the water surface

Direction of travel

Body position flat and streamlined during the glide phase when the face is submerged

The main aim should be good streamlining, however the underwater recovery movements of the arms and legs together with the lifting of the head to breathe, all compromise the overall body position. In order to reduce resistance created by these movements, as the propulsive phase of an arm pull or leg kick takes place, the opposite end of the body remains still and streamlined.

legs

The most important teaching aspect of the legs is that the action is a series of movements that flow together to make one sweeping leg kicking action.

Heels are drawn up towards the seat. Soles face upwards

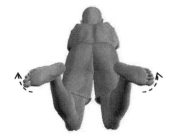

Feet turn outwards to allow the heels and soles to aid propulsion

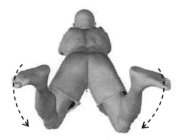

Heels push back and outwards in a whip-like action

It is more important for a swimmer or teacher to recognise the difference between the wedge kick and the whip kick in breaststroke. The leg action provides the largest amount of propulsion in the stroke and swimmers will favour a wedge kick or a whip kick depending on which comes most naturally. For a whip kick, the legs kick in a whip-like action with the knees remaining close together. For a wedge kick the legs kick in a wider, more deliberate circular path.

The leg kick as a whole should be a simultaneous and flowing action, providing the majority of the propulsion. Knees bend as the heels are drawn up towards the seat and toes are turned out ready for the heels and soles of the feet to drive the water backwards. The legs sweep outwards and downwards in a flowing circular path, accelerating as they kick and return together and straight, providing a streamlined position.

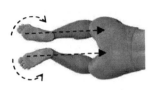

Heels drawn towards the seat and feet turn out

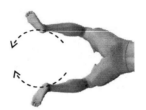

Heels drive back in a circular whip like action giving the kick power and motion

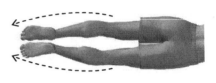

Kick finishes in a streamlined position with legs straight and toes pointed

arms

The amount of propulsion generated from arm techniques has developed over the years as the stroke has changed to become more competitive. The arm action overall provides the smallest propulsive phase of the four competitive strokes.

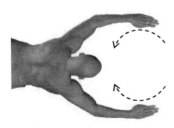

Arms and hands pull around and downwards

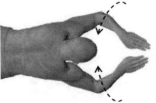

Elbows tuck in and arms and hands stretch forward into a glide

Catch

Arm action begins with the arms fully extended out in front, fingers and hands together. Hands pitch outwards and downwards to an angle of about 45 degrees at the start of the catch phase. Arms pull outwards and downwards until they are approximately shoulder width apart. Elbows begin to bend and shoulders roll inwards at the end of the catch phase.

Propulsive phase

Arms sweep downwards and inwards and the hands pull to their deepest point. Elbows bend to 90 degrees and remain high. At the end of the down sweep, the hands sweep inwards and slightly upwards. Elbows tuck into the sides as the hands are pulled inwards towards the chest and the chin.

Recovery

Hands recover by stretching forwards in a streamlined position. Hands recover under, on or over the water surface, depending on the style of stroke to be taught.

breathing

The stroke action gives a natural body lift which gives the ideal breathing point with each stroke.

Inhalation takes place at the end of the in sweep as the body allows the head to lift clear of the water. The head should be lifted enough for the mouth to clear the surface and inhale, but not excessively so as to keep the frontal resistance created by this movement to a minimum.

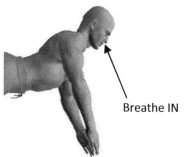

Breathe IN

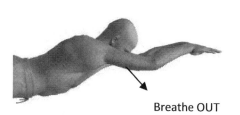

Breathe OUT

Breathing in occurs as the arms pull down and the head rises above the surface

Breathing out occurs as the arms recover out in front

Explosive or trickle breathing can be utilised.

Head returns to the water to exhale as the arms stretch forward to begin their recovery phase.

Some swimmers perform the stroke with the head raised throughout to keep the mouth and nose clear of the water at all times. This simplifies the breathing.

The coordination of the propulsive phases should be a continuous alternating action, where one propulsive phase takes over as one ends. The stroke timing can be summed up with the following sequence: pull, breath, kick, glide.

A streamlined body position at the end of that sequence is essential to capitalise on the propulsive phases of the stroke. The timing can be considered in another way: when the arms are pulling in their propulsive phase, the legs are streamlined and when the legs are kicking in propulsion, the arms are streamlined.

| Body position starts with hands and feet together | Pull, breathe, kick, glide sequence is performed | Swimmer returns to original body position. |

Full body extension is essential before the start of each stroke cycle.

Competitive variations in stroke timing can be found by decreasing or even eliminating the glide and using the arm and leg actions in an almost continuous stroke to give more propulsion.

full stroke overview

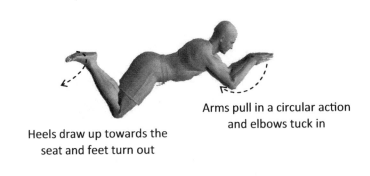

Heels draw up towards the
seat and feet turn out

Arms pull in a circular action
and elbows tuck in

Legs kick backwards
providing power and
propulsion

Arms stretch forward
into a glide

chapter 8

butterfly

butterfly

Butterfly stroke is the most recent stroke, developed in the 1950's, and it is the second fastest stroke to Front Crawl. The stroke evolved from Breaststroke as it also contains a simultaneous leg action and simultaneous arm action. The stroke requires a great deal of upper body strength and can be very physically demanding; therefore it is a stroke that is swum competitively rather than recreationally.

Buoyancy is very important because the arms are recovered over the water the head is raised to breathe, therefore good floaters will achieve this far easier than poor floaters.

The timing and coordination of the stroke is usually a two beat cycle of leg kicks to one arm cycle.

The undulating action of the body and the legs create great demands of the spine, therefore there are many alternative exercises and practices that can be used to make learning the stroke easier and less physical.

body position

The body position varies through the stroke cycle due to the continuous undulating action. The body should undulate from head to toe, producing a dolphin-type action.

Although undulation is unavoidable, the body position should be kept as horizontal as possible to keep frontal resistance to a minimum. Intermittent or alternative breathing will help to maintain this required body position.

The body should be face down (prone) with the crown of the head leading the action.

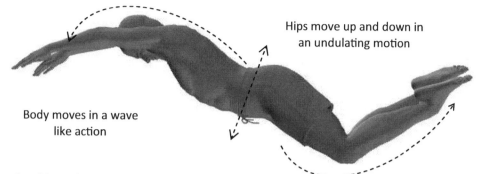

Hips move up and down in an undulating motion

Body moves in a wave like action

The shoulders should remain level throughout and the head should remain central and still, looking down until breathing is required.

Hips should be inline with the shoulders and should remain parallel to the direction of travel.

---

legs

The main functions of butterfly stroke leg action are to balance the arm action and help to provide some propulsion. This action then generates the undulating movement of the body position as the swimmer moves through the water.

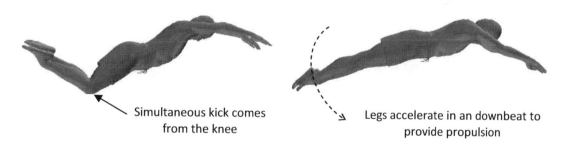

Simultaneous kick comes from the knee

Legs accelerate in an downbeat to provide propulsion

The legs kick simultaneously in an action that is similar to that of front crawl but with a greater and more pronounced knee bend.

The upbeat of the kick should come from the hip and the ankles should be relaxed with toes pointed. The legs move upwards without bending at the knees and the soles of the feet press against the water vertically and backwards.

Knees bend and then straighten on the downbeat to provide propulsion. The legs should accelerate to provide power on the downbeat.

The butterfly stroke arm action is a continuous simultaneous movement that requires significant upper body strength. The action of the arms is similar to that of front crawl and the underwater catch, down sweep and upsweep parts draw the shape of a 'keyhole' through its movement path.

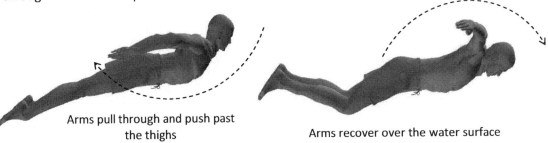

Arms pull through and push past
the thighs

Arms recover over the water surface

Entry

The entry of the hands into the water should be finger tips first, leading with the thumb. Fingers should be together with palms flat and facing outwards. Arms should be stretched forward with a slightly bent elbow. Entry should be with arms extended inline with the shoulders.

Catch and down sweep

The pitch of the hands changes to a deeper angle with hands almost vertical. The catch and down sweep should begin just outside the shoulder line. Palms remain facing in the direction of travel. The elbow should bend to about 90 degrees to provide the extra power required. The hands sweep in a circular movement similar to breaststroke, but in a downwards path.

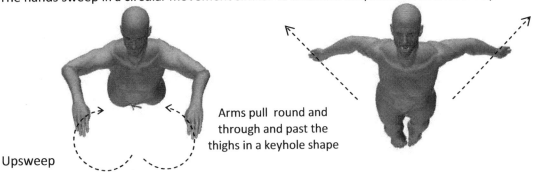

Arms pull round and
through and past the
thighs in a keyhole shape

Upsweep

The pitch of the hands changes to face out and upwards towards the water surface. Elbows extend fully to straighten the arms and hands towards the thighs.

Recovery

Hands and arms must clear the water on recovery in accordance with ASA Law. Arms and hands should exit the water little finger facing upwards. Arms must clear the surface as they are 'thrown' over and forwards. Palms remain facing outwards, naturally giving a thumb-first entry.

Breathing technique during butterfly stroke is a rapid and explosive action.

Inhalation takes place as the arms complete their upsweep and begin to recover, as the body begins to rise. The head is lifted enough for the mouth to clear the water and the chin should be pushed forward, but remain at the water surface. Some exhalation underwater takes place during this phase.

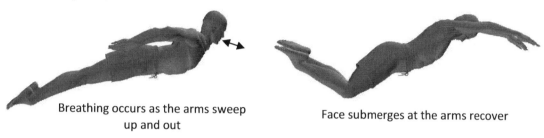

Breathing occurs as the arms sweep up and out

Face submerges at the arms recover

The head is lowered quickly into the water again as the arms recover inline with the shoulders, to resume an overall streamlined position and maintain minimal frontal resistance.

Explosive breathing is normally preferred but a combination of trickle and explosive breathing can be used. Explosive breathing involves a rapid exhalation followed immediately by inhalation, requiring powerful use of the respiratory muscles.

timing

The butterfly stroke cycle should contain 2 leg kicks to 1 arm cycle where the first kick occurs when the arms are forward and the second kick when the have pulled back.

Legs kick downwards as the hands catch and begin to pull

Legs kick again as the arms pull through to the thighs

The downbeat of the first leg kick occurs at the catch and down sweep phase. Both arms will have been in the air during recovery, causing the hips to sink. The subsequent kick should be strong enough to counter balance this hip movement.

The second downbeat leg kick occurs during the powerful and accelerating upsweep phase of the arm cycle. During this movement, the feet react towards the hands and the strength will contribute towards propulsion.

Breathing can occur every stroke cycle or every other stroke cycle.

"The swimmer who says 'it can't be done' is passed by the swimmer who is doing it"
Unknown

chapter 9

stroke exercises

stroke exercises

The next time there are people swimming at the swimming pool, watch them carefully. How many think they are great swimmers? How many are out of breath after just one length? How many are paddling up and down, desperately trying to keep their hair dry?

The fact is people who swim the four basic strokes usually swim badly. Their swimming strokes are usually inefficient, making them use more energy then if they had correct swimming technique.

Front crawl technique usually goes wrong when swimmers hold their breath for as long as they can and then wonder why they get so out of breath. Front crawl breathing technique is made a whole lot easier when arm and leg actions are smooth and efficient.

Breaststroke swimmers usually use their arms far too much, when actually it's the legs that need to provide the majority of the power during the swimming stroke. Some don't even use the legs at all! Those that do, usually fail to turn out their feet and miss out on the power that could be gained from the heels and soles of the feet during the powerful whip action of the kick. There are specific swimming exercises in this section to help correct this.

People that swim backstroke usually lack an efficient leg kick by allowing the legs to sink. This is then compounded by an incorrect body position, with the head too high, making the hips sink and the swimming stroke as a whole inefficient.

Butterfly stroke is arguably the most difficult and the most tiring. Very few people swim butterfly recreationally and instead it is swum competitively. This swimming stroke requires a great deal of power and upper body strength, as well as a powerful leg kick.

Michael Phelps swims butterfly

The stroke exercises contained in the following parts of this book form reference sections for each stroke.

what are they?

Each specific exercise focuses on a certain aspect of the swimming stroke, for example the body position, the leg kick, the arms, the breathing or the timing and coordination, all separated into easy to learn stages. Each one contains a photograph of the exercise being performed, a graphical diagram and all the technique elements and key focus points that are relevant to that particular exercise.

how will they help?

They break down your swimming stroke into its core elements and then force you to focus on that certain area. For example if you are performing a leg kick exercise, the leg kick is isolated and therefore your focus and concentration is only on the legs. The technical information and key focus points then fix your concentration on the most important elements of the leg kick. The result: a more efficient and technically correct leg kick. The same then goes for exercises for the arms, breathing, timing and coordination and so on.

will they improve your swimming strokes?

Yes, definitely! These practical exercises not only isolate certain areas but can highlight your bad habits. Once you've worked though each element of the stroke and practiced the exercises a few times, you will slowly eliminate your bad habits. The result: a more efficient and technically correct swimming stroke, swum with less effort!

how to use this section

The page layout for each exercise follows the same format, keeping all relevant information on one page. The aims, technical focuses and key points are all listed with a photograph and graphical diagram of the exercise.

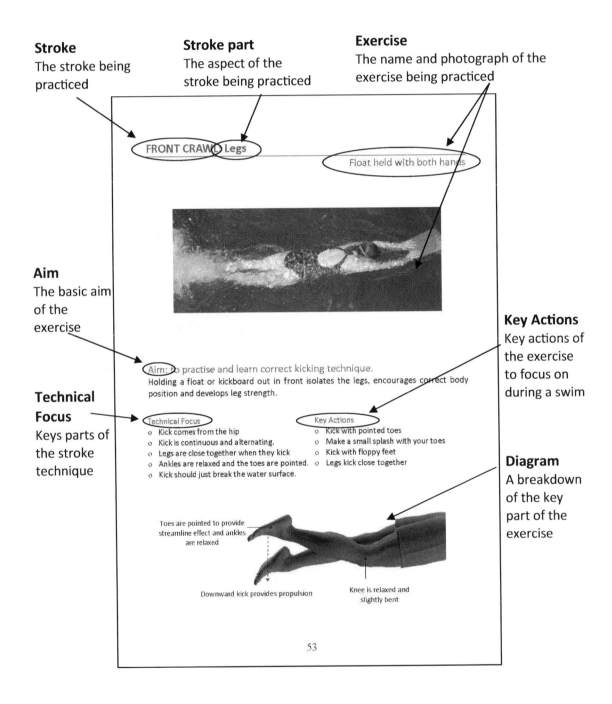

Stroke
The stroke being practiced

Stroke part
The aspect of the stroke being practiced

Exercise
The name and photograph of the exercise being practiced

FRONT CRAWL Legs

Float held with both hands

Aim
The basic aim of the exercise

Key Actions
Key actions of the exercise to focus on during a swim

Aim: To practise and learn correct kicking technique.
Holding a float or kickboard out in front isolates the legs, encourages correct body position and develops leg strength.

Technical Focus
Keys parts of the stroke technique

Technical Focus
o Kick comes from the hip
o Kick is continuous and alternating.
o Legs are close together when they kick
o Ankles are relaxed and the toes are pointed.
o Kick should just break the water surface.

Key Actions
o Kick with pointed toes
o Make a small splash with your toes
o Kick with floppy feet
o Legs kick close together

Diagram
A breakdown of the key part of the exercise

Toes are pointed to provide streamline effect and ankles are relaxed

Downward kick provides propulsion

Knee is relaxed and slightly bent

53

front crawl

stroke exercises

Holding the poolside

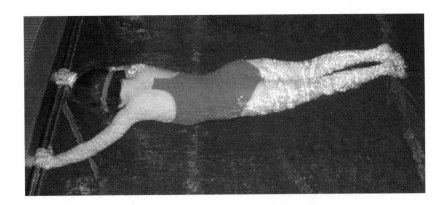

Aim: to encourage confidence in a floating position.

The swimmer holds the poolside for added security and some assistance may be required as some people will not naturally float.

Technical Focus

o Head is central and still
o Face is submerged
o Eyes are looking downwards
o Shoulders should be level
o Hips are close to the surface
o Legs are together and in line with the body

Key Actions

o Relax
o Keep the head tucked between the arms
o Stretch out as far as you can
o Keep your feet together

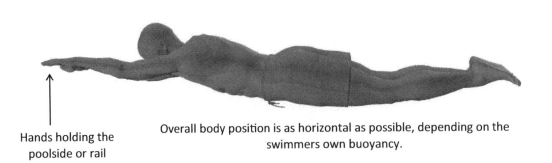

Hands holding the poolside or rail

Overall body position is as horizontal as possible, depending on the swimmers own buoyancy.

FRONT CRAWL: Body Position

Static practice holding floats

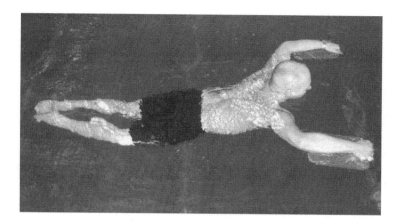

Aim: to help the swimmer develop confidence in his/her own buoyancy.
A float can be held under each arm or a single float held out in front, depending on levels of confidence and ability. Some swimmers may need extra assistance if they lack natural buoyancy.

Technical Focus
o   Head is central and still
o   Face is submerged
o   Eyes are looking downwards
o   Shoulders should be level
o   Hips are close to the surface
o   Legs are together and in line with the body

Key Actions
o   Relax
o   Keep the head tucked between the arms
o   Stretch out as far as you can
o   Keep your feet together

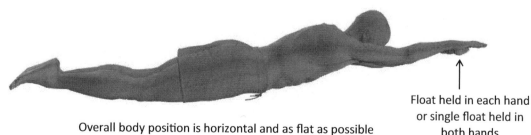

Overall body position is horizontal and as flat as possible

Float held in each hand or single float held in both hands

FRONT CRAWL: Body Position

Push and glide from standing

 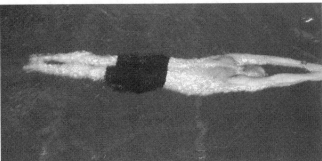

Aim: to develop correct body position and confidence in pushing off.

The swimmer can start with arms stretched out in front and pushes off from the pool floor or from the wall with one foot and glides through the water unaided.

Technical Focus

o Initial push should be enough to gain good movement
o Head remains still and central
o Face submerged so that the water is at brow level
o Shoulders should be level
o Legs in line with the body

Key Actions

o Push hard from the side/pool floor
o Keep your head tucked between your arms
o Stretch out as far as you can
o Keep your hands together
o Keep your feet together

Direction of travel

Legs push off from pool
side or pool floor

FRONT CRAWL: Body Position

Push and glide from the side holding floats

Aim: to develop correct body position whilst moving through the water.
Body position should be laying prone with the head up at this stage. The use of floats helps to build confidence, particularly in the weak or nervous swimmer.   The floats create a slight resistance to the glide, but this is still a useful exercise.

Technical Focus
o   Head remains still and central with the chin on the water surface
o   Eyes are looking forwards and downwards
o   Shoulders should be level and square
o   Hips are close to the surface
o   Legs are in line with the body

Key Actions
o   Push hard from the wall
o   Relax and float across the water
o   Keep your head still and look forward
o   Stretch out as far as you can
o   Keep your feet together

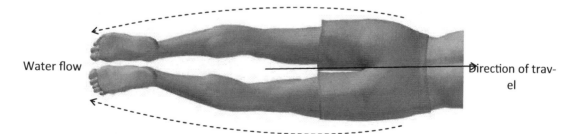

Water flow

Direction of travel

Streamlined body position minimises drag allowing efficient movement through the water

FRONT CRAWL: Body Position

Push and glide from the poolside

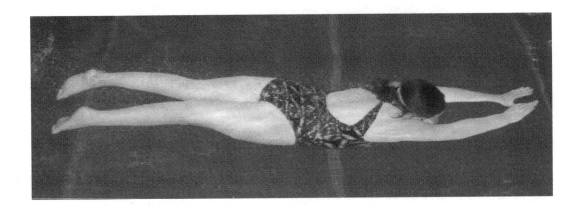

Aim: to develop a streamlined body position whilst moving thorough the water.

Movement is created by pushing and gliding from holding position at the poolside.

Technical Focus
- o Head remains still and central
- o Face submerged so that the water is at brow level
- o Shoulders should be level and square
- o Legs are in line with the body
- o Overall body position should be stream-lined

Key Actions
- o Push hard from the side
- o Stretch your arms out in front as you push
- o Keep your head tucked between your arms
- o Stretch out as far as you can
- o Keep your hands and feet together

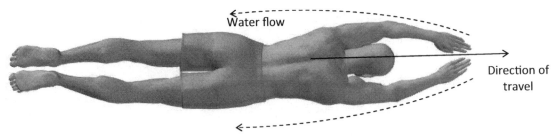

Streamlined body position minimises drag, allowing efficient movement through the water

FRONT CRAWL: Legs

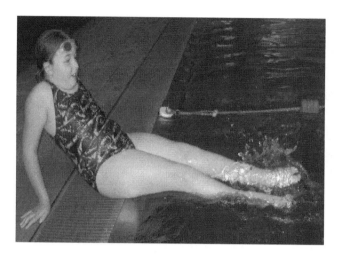

Aim: to give the swimmer the feel of the water during the kick.

Sitting on pool side kicking is an ideal exercise for the beginner to practise correct leg kicking action with the added confidence of sitting on the poolside.

Technical Focus
o Kick is continuous and alternating
o Knee is only slightly bent
o Legs are close together when they kick
o Ankles are relaxed and the toes are pointed.

Key Actions
o Kick with straight legs
o Pointed toes
o Make a small splash with your toes
o Kick with floppy feet
o Kick continuously

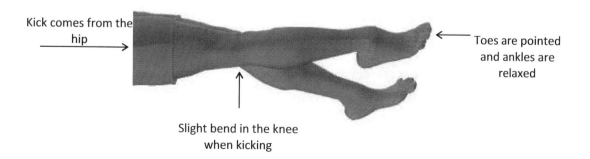

Kick comes from the hip

Toes are pointed and ankles are relaxed

Slight bend in the knee when kicking

FRONT CRAWL: Legs

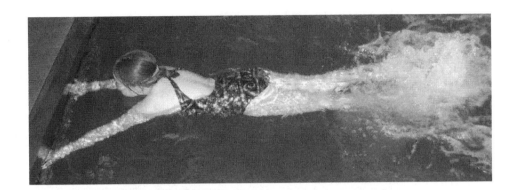

Aim: to encourage the swimmer to learn the kicking action.

Holding the poolside enhances confidence and helps develop leg strength and technique.

Technical Focus

o Kick comes from the hip
o Kick is continuous and alternating
o Knee is only slightly bent
o Legs are close together when they kick
o Ankles are relaxed and the toes are pointed
o Kick should just break the water surface

Key Actions

o Kick with straight legs
o Pointed toes
o Make a small splash with your toes
o Kick with floppy feet
o Kick from your hips
o Kick continuously
o Legs kick close together

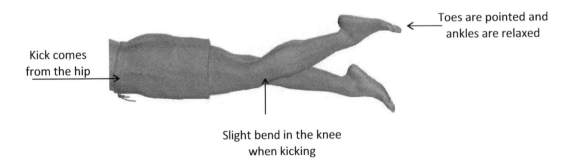

Toes are pointed and ankles are relaxed

Kick comes from the hip

Slight bend in the knee when kicking

FRONT CRAWL: Legs

Legs kick with a float held under each arm

Aim: to learn correct kicking technique and develop leg strength.

The added stability of two floats will help boost confidence in the weak swimmer.

Technical Focus

o   Kick comes from the hip
o   Kick is continuous and alternating
o   Chin remains on the water surface
o   Legs are close together when they kick
o   Ankles are relaxed and the toes are pointed
o   Kick should just break the water surface
o   Upper body and arms should be relaxed

Key Actions

o   Kick with straight legs
o   Pointed toes
o   Kick with floppy feet
o   Kick from your hips
o   Kick continuously

Toes are pointed to provide streamline effect and ankles are relaxed

Downward kick provides propulsion

FRONT CRAWL: Legs

Float held with both hands

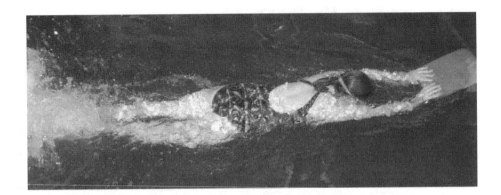

Aim: to practise and learn correct kicking technique.

Holding a float or kickboard out in front isolates the legs, encourages correct body position and develops leg strength.

Technical Focus
o   Kick comes from the hip
o   Kick is continuous and alternating.
o   Legs are close together when they kick
o   Ankles are relaxed and the toes are pointed.
o   Kick should just break the water surface.

Key Actions
o   Kick with pointed toes
o   Make a small splash with your toes
o   Kick with floppy feet
o   Legs kick close together

Toes are pointed to provide streamline effect and ankles are relaxed

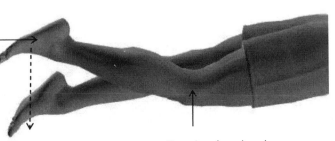

Downward kick provides propulsion

Knee is relaxed and slightly bent

68

FRONT CRAWL: Legs

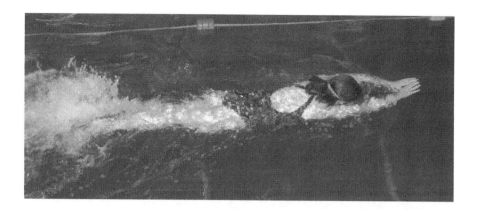

Aim: to develop correct body position and leg kick whilst holding the breath.

Push and glide without a float and add a leg kick whilst maintaining a streamlined body position.

Technical Focus

o Kick comes from the hip
o Streamlined body position is maintained
o Kick is continuous and alternating
o Legs are close together when they kick
o Ankles are relaxed and the toes are pointed
o Kick should just break the water surface

Key Actions

o Kick with straight legs and pointed toes
o Kick with floppy feet
o Kick from your hips
o Kick continuously

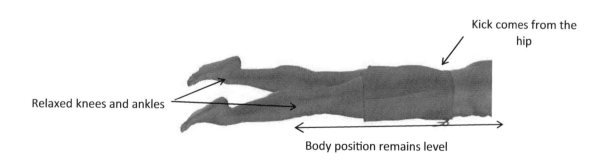

Kick comes from the hip

Relaxed knees and ankles

Body position remains level

FRONT CRAWL: Legs

Leg kick whilst holding a float vertically in front

Aim: to create resistance and help develop strength and stamina.

Holding a float vertically in front increases the intensity of the kicking action which in turn develops leg strength and stamina.

Technical Focus
o Kick comes from the hip
o Streamlined body position is maintained
o Kick is continuous and alternating
o Legs are close together when they kick
o Ankles are relaxed and the toes are pointed
o Kick should just break the water surface

Key Actions
o Kick with straight legs and pointed toes
o Kick with floppy feet
o Kick from your hips
o Kick continuously

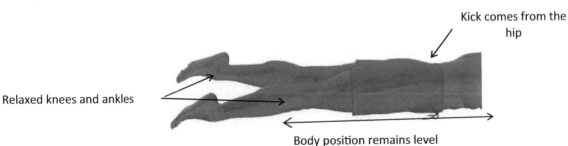

Kick comes from the hip

Relaxed knees and ankles

Body position remains level

FRONT CRAWL: Arms

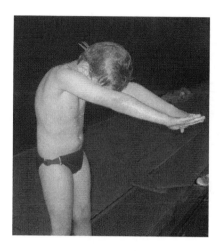 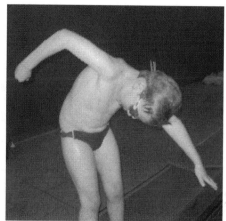

Aim: to practise correct arm movement whilst in a static position.

This is an exercise for beginners that can be practised on the poolside or standing in shallow water.

Technical Focus
- Fingers should be together
- Pull through to the hips
- Elbow bends and leads upwards

Key Actions
- Keep your fingers together
- Continuous smooth action
- Brush your hand past your thigh
- Gradually bend your elbow

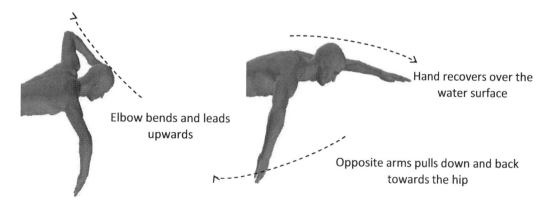

Elbow bends and leads upwards

Hand recovers over the water surface

Opposite arms pulls down and back towards the hip

FRONT CRAWL: Arms

Single arm practice with float held in one hand

Aim: to practise and improve correct arm technique

This practice allows the swimmer to develop arm technique whilst maintaining body position and leg kick. Holding a float with one hand gives the weaker swimmer security and allows the competent swimmer to focus on a single arm.

Technical Focus
o Fingertips enter first with thumb side down
o Fingers should be together
o Pull should be an elongated 'S' shape
o Pull through to the hips
o Elbow exits the water first
o Fingers clear the water on recovery

Key Actions
o Keep your fingers together
o Brush your hand past your thigh
o Pull fast under the water
o Make an 'S' shape under the water
o Elbow out first
o Reach over the water surface

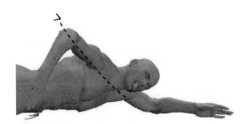

Elbow leads out of the water first

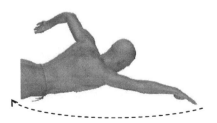

Arm pulls back through the water towards the hip

FRONT CRAWL: Arms

Alternating arm pull whilst holding a float out in front

Aim: to develop coordination and correct arm pull technique.

The swimmer uses an alternating arm action. This also introduces a timing aspect as the leg kick has to be continuous at the same time.

Technical Focus
o Clean entry with fingertips first and thumb side down
o Fingers should be together
o Each arm pulls through to the hips
o Elbow leads out first
o Fingers clear the water on recovery

Key Actions
o Finger tips in first
o Brush your hand past your thigh
o Pull fast under the water
o Elbow out first
o Reach over the water surface

Arm pulls through towards the hip

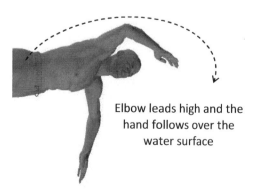

Elbow leads high and the hand follows over the water surface

Arm action using a pull-buoy

Aim: to develop arm pull strength, technique and coordination.

This is a more advanced exercise which requires stamina and a degree of breathing technique.

Technical Focus
o Fingertips enter first with thumb side down
o Fingers should be together
o Pull should be an elongated 'S' shape
o Pull through to the hips
o Elbow comes out first
o Fingers clear the water on recovery

Key Actions
o Long strokes
o Smooth continuous action
o Brush your hand past your thigh
o Make an 'S' shape under the water
o Elbow out first
o Reach over the water surface

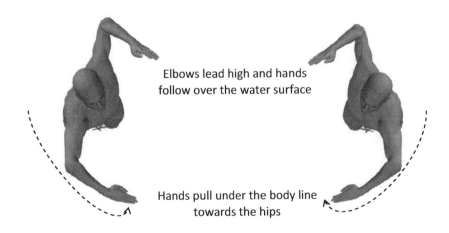

Elbows lead high and hands follow over the water surface

Hands pull under the body line towards the hips

FRONT CRAWL: Arms

Push and glide adding arm cycles

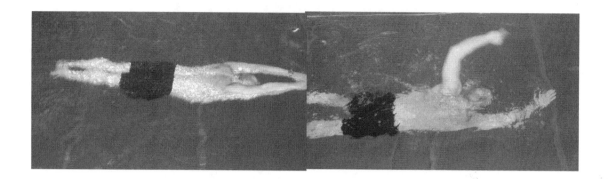

Aim: to combine correct arm action with a streamlined body position.
The swimmer performs a push and glide to establish body position and then adds arm cycles, whilst maintaining body position.

Technical Focus
o Clean entry with fingertips first
o Pull should be an elongated 'S' shape
o Pull through to the hips
o Elbow comes out first
o Fingers clear the water on recovery

Key Actions
o Finger tips in the water first
o Brush your hand past your thigh
o Make an 'S' shape under the water
o Elbow out first
o Reach over the water surface

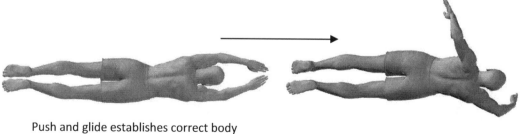

Push and glide establishes correct body position

Arm cycles are added

FRONT CRAWL: Breathing

Aim: to practice and develop breathing technique.

The pupil stands and holds the pool rail with one arm extended, breathing to one side to introduce the beginner to breathing whilst having his/her face submerged.

Technical Focus

o Breathing should be from the mouth
o Breathing in should be when the head is turned to the side
o Breathing out should be when the face is down

Key Actions

o Breathe out through your mouth
o Blow out slowly and gently
o Turn your head to the side when you breathe in
o See how long you can make the breath last

BREATHE IN

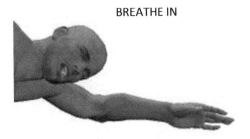

Head turns to the side and mouth clears the water surface

BREATHE OUT

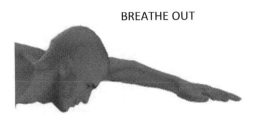

Head faces forward and down

FRONT CRAWL: Breathing

Holding a float in front with diagonal grip

Aim: to encourage correct breathing technique whilst kicking.

The float is held in front, one arm extended fully, the other holding the near corner with elbow low. This creates a gap for the head and mouth to be turned in at the point of breathing.

Technical Focus
o Breathing should be from the mouth
o Breathing in should be when the head is turned to the side
o Breathing out should be slow and controlled

Key Actions
o Turn head towards the bent arm to breathe
o Breathe out through your mouth
o Blow out slowly and gently
o Return head to the centre soon after breathing

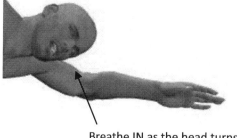

Breathe IN as the head turns out of the water

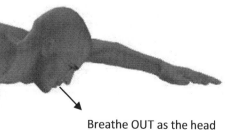

Breathe OUT as the head faces forward and down

FRONT CRAWL: Breathing

Float held in one hand, arm action with breathing

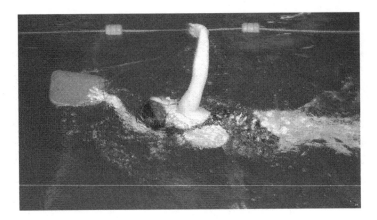

Aim: to develop correct breathing technique whilst pulling with one arm.

This allows the swimmer to add the arm action to the breathing technique and perfect the timing of the two movements. The float provides support and keeps the exercise as a simple single arm practice.

Technical Focus

o Head moves enough for mouth to clear the water
o Breathing in occurs when the head is turned to the side
o Breathing out should be slow
o Breathing should be from the mouth

Key Actions

o Turn head to the side of the pulling arm
o Breathe out through your mouth
o Blow out slowly and gently
o Return head to the centre soon after breathing

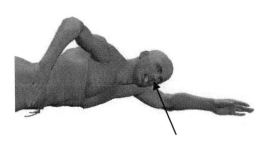
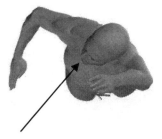

Breath IN as the arm pulls through and the head turns to the side

FRONT CRAWL: Breathing

Float held in both hands, alternate arm pull with breathing

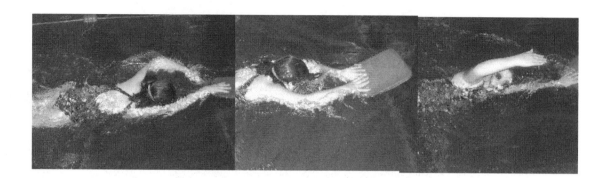

Aim: to practise bi-lateral breathing with the support of a float held out in front.

A single float is held in both hands and one arm pull is performed at a time with the head turning to breathe with each arm pull. Different arm action and breathing cycles can be used, for example; breathe every other arm pull or every three arm pulls.

Technical Focus

o Head should be still when not taking a breath
o Head movement should be minimal enough for mouth to clear the water
o Breathing in should be when the head is turned to the side
o Breathing should be from the mouth

Key Actions

o Keep head still until you need to breathe
o Breathe every 3 strokes (or another pattern you may choose)
o Turn head to the side as your arm pulls back
o Return head to the centre soon after breathing
o Breathe out through your mouth

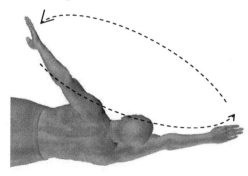

Head turns to the left side as the left arm pulls through and begins to recover

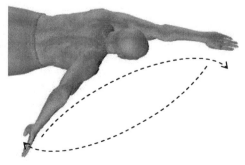

Head turns to the right side as the right arm pulls through and begins to recover

Front crawl catch up

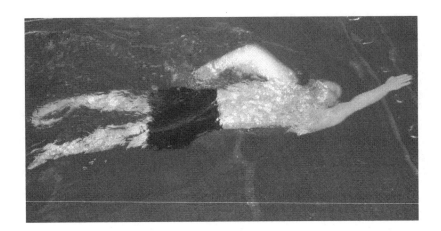

Aim: to practice correct stroke timing and develop coordination.

The opposite arm remains stationary until the arm performing the pull recovers to its starting position. This is an advanced exercise and encourages the swimmer to maintain body position and leg kick whilst practicing arm cycles.

Technical Focus
o Clean entry with fingertips first
o Pull should be an elongated 'S' shape
o Pull through to the hips
o Elbow comes out first
o Fingers clear the water on recovery

Key Actions
o Finger tips in the water first
o Brush your hand past your thigh
o Make an 'S' shape under the water
o Elbow out first
o Reach over the water surface

Legs kick and hands are held together

One arm pulls and recovers as the opposite arm remains in front

Arm recovers to its position in front before the opposite arm pulls and recovers

FRONT CRAWL

Aim: full stroke Front Crawl demonstrating correct leg action, arm action, breathing and timing.

Technical Focus
o Stroke is smooth and continuous
o Head in line with the body
o Legs in line with the body
o Head remains still
o Leg kick is continuous and alternating
o Arm action is continuous and alternating
o Breathing is regular and to the side
o Stroke ideally has a 6 beat cycle

Key Actions
o Keep your head still until you breathe
o Kick continuously from your hips
o Stretch forward with each arm action
o Pull continuously under your body
o Count 3 leg kicks with each arm pull

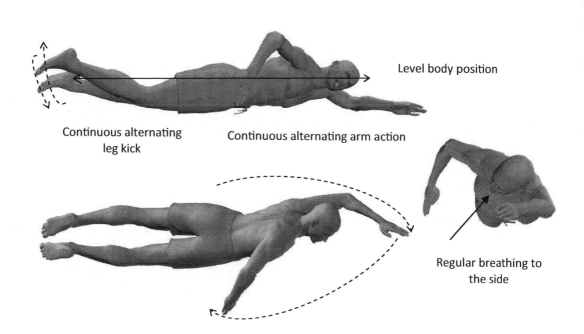

Level body position

Continuous alternating leg kick

Continuous alternating arm action

Regular breathing to the side

Front Crawl

Exercise quick reference guide

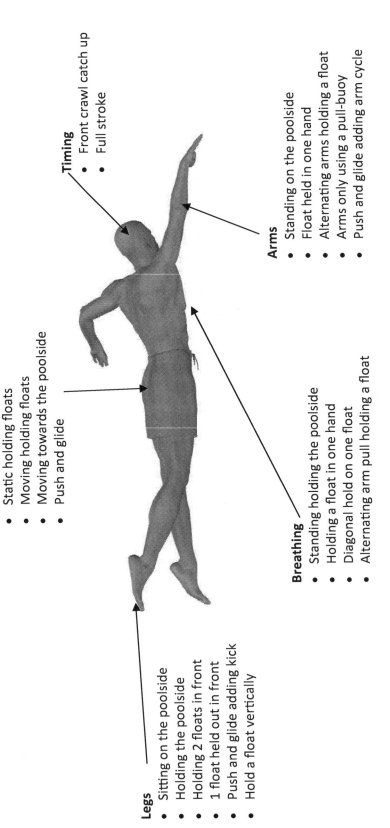

Body Position
- Holding the poolside
- Static holding floats
- Moving holding floats
- Moving towards the poolside
- Push and glide

Timing
- Front crawl catch up
- Full stroke

Arms
- Standing on the poolside
- Float held in one hand
- Alternating arms holding a float
- Arms only using a pull-buoy
- Push and glide adding arm cycle

Breathing
- Standing holding the poolside
- Holding a float in one hand
- Diagonal hold on one float
- Alternating arm pull holding a float

Legs
- Sitting on the poolside
- Holding the poolside
- Holding 2 floats in front
- 1 float held out in front
- Push and glide adding kick
- Hold a float vertically

backstroke

stroke exercises

BACKSTROKE: Body Position

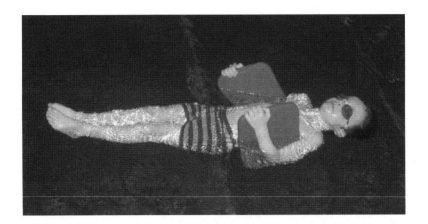

Aim: to gain confidence in a supine position on the water surface.

This exercise is ideal for the nervous swimmer. Support initially can be provided by the teacher, if he/she is also in the water. Support can then be provided by 2 floats, one placed under each arm, or by a woggle placed under both arms as in the photograph above.

Technical Focus

o Overall body should be horizontal and streamlined
o Head remains still
o Eyes looking upwards and towards the feet
o Hips must be close to the surface
o Legs must be together

Key Actions

o Relax
o Make your body flat on top of the water
o Keep your head back
o Push your tummy up to the surface
o Look up to the ceiling
o Keep your head still
o Keep yourself in a long straight line

Body position remains level

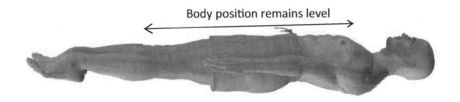

BACKSTROKE: Body Position

Static supine position, holding a single float

Aim: to develop confidence in a supine position.

Holding a single float across the chest gives security to the nervous swimmer, but is not as stable as a woggle or a float under each arm and so is a subtle and gradual progression. If necessary, this exercise can be performed without a float, as shown in the diagram below, as an additional progression.

Technical Focus
o Overall body should be horizontal
o Head remains still
o Eyes looking upwards
o Hips must be close to the surface
o Legs must be together

Key Actions
o Relax
o Keep your head back
o Push your tummy up to the surface
o Look up to the ceiling
o Keep your head still

Body position remains horizontal and relaxed

BACKSTROKE: Body Position

Push and glide holding a float

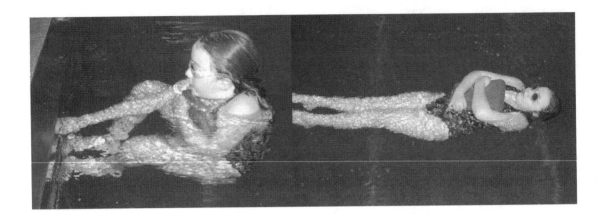

Aim: to gain confidence and move through the water in a supine position.

Holding a float gives added security to the nervous or weak swimmer whilst helping to maintain correct body position.

Technical Focus
- Overall body should be horizontal and streamlined
- Head remains still
- Eyes looking upwards
- Hips must be close to the surface
- Legs must be together

Key Actions
- Relax
- Keep your head back and chin up
- Push your tummy up to the surface
- Look up to the ceiling
- Keep your head still
- Push off like a rocket

Body position remains level

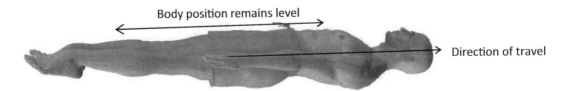

Direction of travel

Float can be placed on the chest or behind the head as in the photos above.

BACKSTROKE: Body Position

Push and glide from the poolside without floats

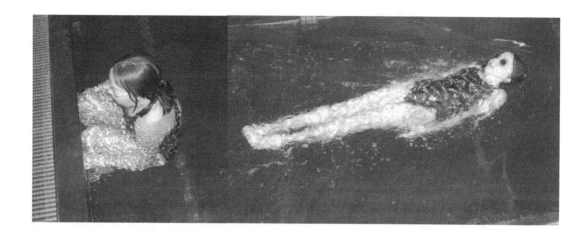

Aim: to encourage correct body position whilst moving.

The swimmer uses the momentum of a push from the pool side. Arms are held by the sides or held straight over the head in more advanced cases.

Technical Focus
o Overall body should be horizontal and streamlined
o Head remains still
o Eyes looking upwards and towards the feet
o Hips must be close to the surface
o Legs must be together
o Arms are held by the sides

Key Actions
o Relax
o Make your body as long as you can
o Push off like a rocket
o Push your tummy up to the surface
o Look up to the ceiling
o Glide in a long straight line

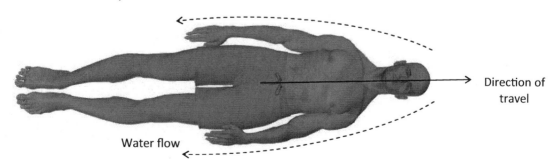

Water flow

Direction of travel

BACKSTROKE: Legs

Static practice, sitting on the poolside

Aim: to develop an alternating leg kick action.

The swimmers is positioned sitting on the pool side with feet in the water. Ideal for the nervous beginner to get accustomed to the 'feel' of the water.

Technical Focus
o Kick comes from the hips
o Toes are pointed
o Legs are together
o Slight knee bend
o Ankles are relaxed

Key Actions
o Point your toes like a ballerina
o Kick from your hips
o Kick with floppy feet
o Keep your legs together
o Make your legs as long as possible

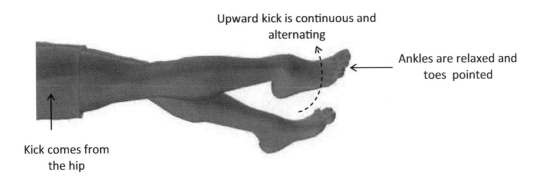

Upward kick is continuous and alternating

Ankles are relaxed and toes pointed

Kick comes from the hip

BACKSTROKE: Legs

Aim: to practise and develop correct leg kick action.

This exercise is ideal for the nervous beginner as an introduction to swimming on the back. The stability of the woggle encourages kicking and motion backwards with ease.

Technical Focus
- o Kick comes from the hips
- o Kick is alternating and continuous
- o Kick breaks the water surface
- o Hips and tummy up near the surface
- o Toes are pointed and ankles relaxed
- o Legs are together
- o Slight knee bend

Key Actions
- o Point your toes like a ballerina
- o Kick from your hips
- o Kick with floppy feet
- o Make a small splash with your toes

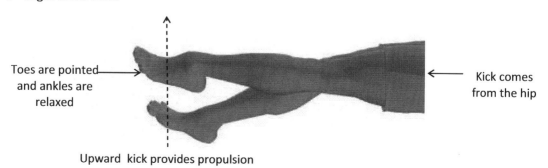

Toes are pointed and ankles are relaxed

Kick comes from the hip

Upward kick provides propulsion

BACKSTROKE: Legs

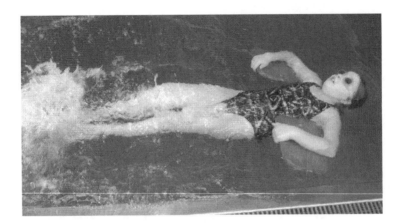

Aim: to practise and develop leg action whilst maintaining correct body position.

Two floats provide good support and encourage a relaxed body position, without creating excessive resistance through the water.

Technical Focus
- o Kick breaks the water surface
- o Hips and tummy are up near the surface
- o Toes are pointed and ankles relaxed
- o Legs are together
- o Slight knee bend
- o Ankles are relaxed

Key Actions
- o Relax and kick hard
- o Point your toes like a ballerina
- o Kick from your hips
- o Kick with floppy feet
- o Make a small splash with your toes
- o Keep your legs together

Body alignment and direction of travel

Continuous alternating upward kick provides propulsion through the water

BACKSTROKE: Legs

Aim: to allow the correct body position to be maintained whilst the legs kick.

This is a progression from having a float held under each arm. The swimmer is less stable but still has the security of one float held on the chest.

Technical Focus
o   Kick comes from the hips
o   Kick is alternating and continuous
o   Kick breaks the water surface
o   Hips and tummy up near the surface
o   Legs are together
o   Ankles are relaxed and toes pointed

Key Actions
o   Point your toes like a ballerina
o   Kick from your hips
o   Kick with floppy feet
o   Make a small splash with your toes
o   Keep your legs together

Ankles are relaxed and toes pointed to provide power to the upward kick

Body position remains level

Kick comes from the hip

BACKSTROKE: Legs

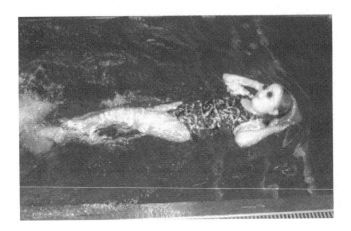

Aim: to encourage correct body position as the legs kick.

The float behind the head helps to keep the chest and hips high. A variation of the exercise with the float held on the chest, this exercise helps to develop leg strength and stamina.

Technical Focus
o   Kick comes from the hips
o   Kick breaks the water surface
o   Hips and tummy up near the surface
o   Toes are pointed and ankles relaxed
o   Legs are together

Key Actions
o   Kick from your hips
o   Kick with floppy feet
o   Make a small splash with your toes
o   Keep your legs together

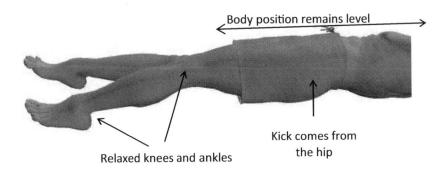

Body position remains level

Relaxed knees and ankles

Kick comes from the hip

BACKSTROKE: Legs

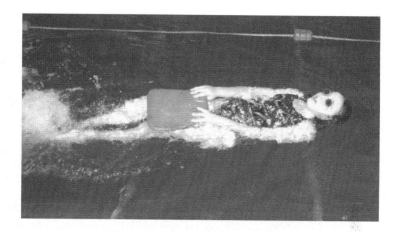

Aim: to prevent excessive knee bend by holding a float over the knees.
This kicking practice should be performed with the float held on the water surface without the knees hitting it as they kick.

Technical Focus
o Kick comes from the hips
o Legs kick without touching the float
o Kick breaks the water surface
o Hips and tummy up near the surface
o Toes are pointed and ankles relaxed

Key Actions
o Kick with straight legs
o Point your toes like a ballerina
o Stop your knees hitting the float
o Kick with floppy feet

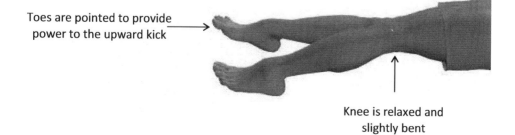

Toes are pointed to provide power to the upward kick

Knee is relaxed and slightly bent

BACKSTROKE: Legs

Float held overhead with arms straight

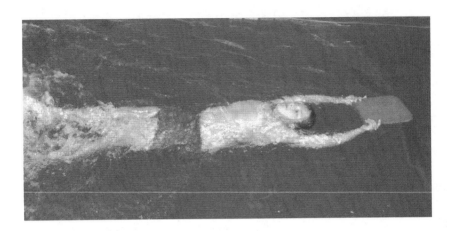

Aim: to enhance a correct body position whilst kicking.

This exercise is a progression from previous leg kick exercises and helps to develop a stronger leg kick.

Technical Focus

o   Kick comes from the hips
o   Arms remain either side of the head
o   Kick breaks the water surface
o   Hips and tummy up near the surface

Key Actions

o   Push your hips and chest up to the surface
o   Point your toes like a ballerina
o   Make your whole body long and straight
o   Kick from your hips
o   Stretch out and kick hard

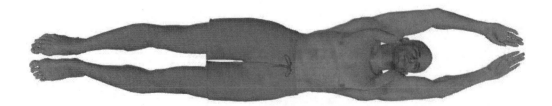

Legs kick and correct body position is maintained throughout.
Note: advanced alternative is shown without holding a float.

BACKSTROKE: Legs

Kicking with arms by the sides, hands sculling

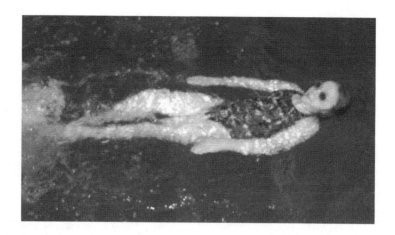

Aim: to practise kicking and maintaining correct body position on the back.

The sculling hand action provides balance and enhances confidence.

Technical Focus
o Kick comes from the hips
o Kick is alternating and continuous
o Kick breaks the water surface
o Hips and tummy up near the surface
o Ankles are relaxed and toes are pointed

Key Actions
o Relax
o Push your hips and chest up to the surface
o Point your toes like a ballerina
o Kick with floppy feet
o Look up to the sky

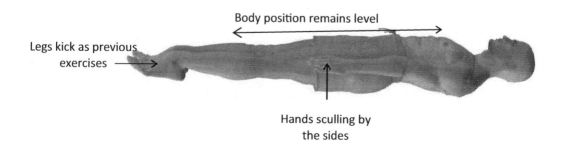

Body position remains level

Legs kick as previous exercises

Hands sculling by the sides

BACKSTROKE: Arms

Aim: to practise the arm action in its most basic form.

Standing on the poolside allows the swimmer to develop basic technique in a static position.

Technical Focus

o Arm action is continuous
o Arms stretch all the way up and brush past the ear
o Arms pull down to the side, towards the hip

Key Actions

o Arms brush past your ear
o Fingers closed together
o Arms are continuous
o Stretch your arm all the way up to your ear
o Pull down to your side

Arm rises upwards, little finger leading and arm brushing the ear

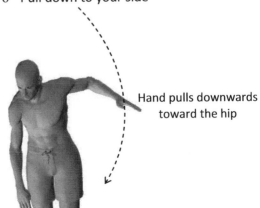

Hand pulls downwards toward the hip

BACKSTROKE: Arms

Single arm pull with a float held on the chest

Aim: to develop correct arm action whilst kicking.

The float held on the chest provides support for the beginner and the single arm action allows easy learning without compromising the swimmer's coordination.

Technical Focus
o Arm action is continuous
o Arms stretch all the way up and brush past the ear
o Arms pull down to the thigh
o Fingers are together
o Little finger enters water first

Key Actions
o Arm brushes past your ear
o Pull down to your thigh
o Fingers closed together
o Little finger enters the water first

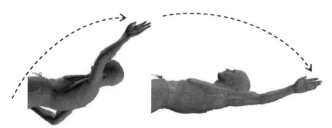

Arm exits the water and brushes past the ear, entering the water little finger first

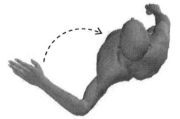

Arm is bent as it pulls through and straightens as it pulls to the thigh

BACKSTROKE: Arms

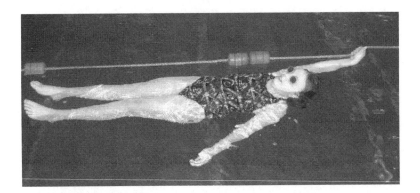

Aim: to develop a bent arm pull using the lane rope to move though the water.

The hand remains fixed on the lane rope as the body is pulled along in the line of the rope. This simulates the bent arm pull action.

Technical Focus
o   Arm action is continuous
o   Arms stretch all the way up and brush past the ear
o   Arms pull down to the thigh
o   Arm action is continuous
o   Thumb comes out first

Key Actions
o   Use the rope to pull you along
o   Arms brush past your ear
o   Stretch over and hold the rope behind
o   Pull fast down the rope
o   Thumb comes out first
o   Little finger enters the water first

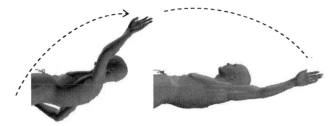

Arm exits the water and brushes past the ear, entering the water little finger first, taking hold of the lane rope

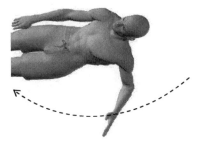

Swimmer pulls from above the head and then pushes past the hip to simulate the bent arm pull action

BACKSTROKE: Arms

Single arm pull with the opposite arm held by the side

Aim: to practise correct arm action without the aid of floats.

This single arm exercise allows focus on one arm whilst the arm held by the side encourages correct body position.

Technical Focus
o Arm action is continuous
o Arms stretch all the way up and brush past the ear
o Arms pull down to the thigh
o Shoulders rock with each arm pull
o Little finger enters the water first

Key Actions
o Arms brush past your ear
o Arms are continuous
o Pull down to your side
o Pull fast through the water
o Little finger enters the water first

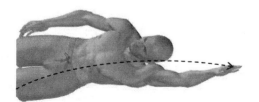

Arm rises upwards, little finger leading and arm brushing the ear

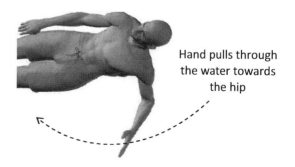

Hand pulls through the water towards the hip

BACKSTROKE: Arms

Aim: to develop a continual arm action using both arms.

The pull-buoy provides support and helps to isolate the arms by preventing the leg kick action. Note: it is normal for the legs to 'sway' from side to side during this exercise.

Technical Focus

o Arm action is continuous and steady
o Arms stretch all the way over and brush past the ear
o Arms pull down to the thigh
o Shoulders rock evenly side to side

Key Actions

o Arms brush past your ear
o Fingers closed together
o Continuous arm action
o Pull hard through the water and down to your side
o Allow your legs to 'sway' side to side

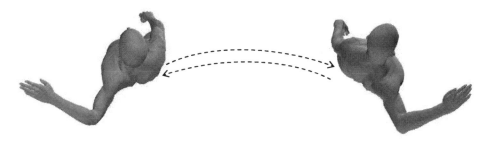

Continual arm action causes an even rocking of the shoulders

Full stroke with breathing

Aim: to focus on breathing in time with the stroke actions.

The swimmer should breathe in and out in regular rhythm with the arm action. This exercise can be incorporated into any of the previous arm action exercises, depending on the ability of the swimmer.

Teacher's Focus

o   Breathing should be regular and rhythmical

Key Actions

o   Breathe in time with your arms
o   Breathe in with one arm pull and out with the other

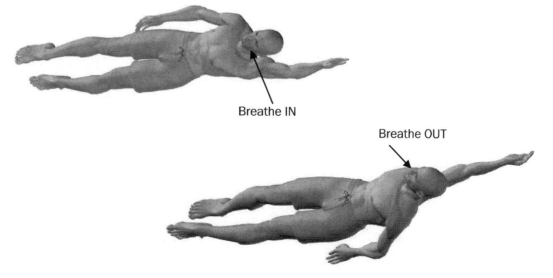

Breathe IN

Breathe OUT

Push and glide adding arms and legs

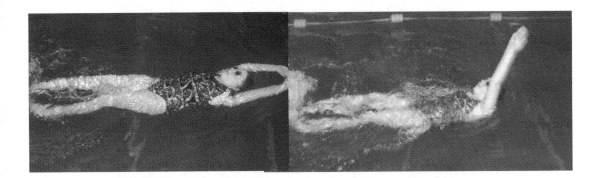

Aim: to practise and develop coordination and stroke timing.

The swimmer performs a push and glide to establish correct body position, then adds arm and leg actions.

Technical Focus

o 3 leg kicks per arm pull
o Leg kick should be continuous
o Arm action should be regular

Key Points

o Count in your head to 3 with each arm pull
o Kick 3 times with each arm pull
o Keep the arm pull continuous
o Keep the leg kick continuous

One arm exits the water as the other begins to pull and the leg kick remains continuous

Aim: to demonstrate full stroke backstroke showing continuous and alternating arm and leg actions, with correct timing, resulting in a smooth and efficient stroke.

Technical Focus
- o Body position should be horizontal and flat
- o Leg kick should be continuous and alternating
- o Arm action is continuous
- o Leg kick breaks the water surface
- o 3 legs kicks per arm pull

Key Actions
- o Kick from your hips
- o Relax
- o Keep your hips and tummy at the surface
- o Make a small splash with your toes
- o Continuous arm action
- o Arms brush past your ear and pull to your side

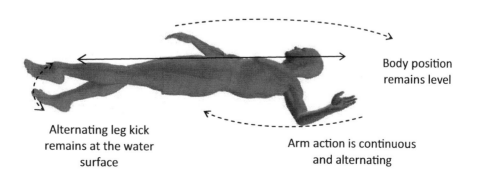

Body position remains level

Alternating leg kick remains at the water surface

Arm action is continuous and alternating

Backstroke

Exercise quick reference guide

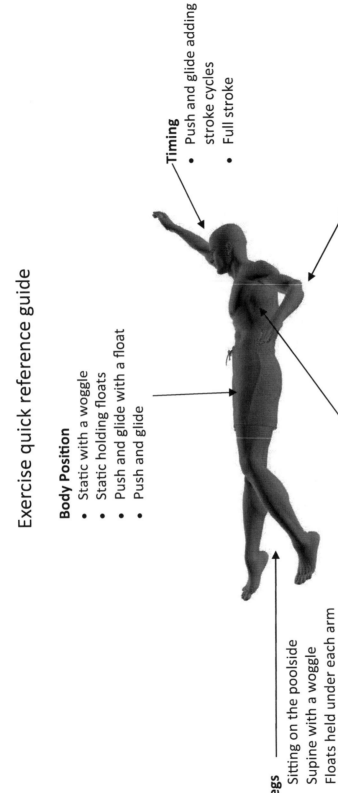

Body Position
- Static with a woggle
- Static holding floats
- Push and glide with a float
- Push and glide

Legs
- Sitting on the poolside
- Supine with a woggle
- Floats held under each arm
- One float held under the head
- Float held on the chest
- Float held with arms extended
- Float held over the knees
- No float, arms held by sides

Breathing
- Full stroke

Timing
- Push and glide adding stroke cycles
- Full stroke

Arms
- Standing on the poolside
- One arm with float held on the chest
- Arms only with pull-buoy
- Bent arm pull holding lane rope

breaststroke

stroke exercises

BREASTSTROKE: Body Position

 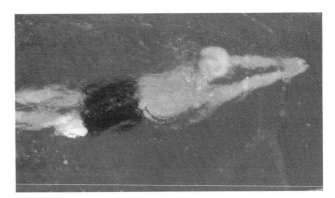

Aim: to develop a basic body position by pushing from the side

The distance of the glide will be limited due to the resistance created by the chest and shoulders. The exercise can be performed with the face submerged as it would be during the glide phase of the stroke or with the head up facing forwards.

Technical Focus

o Head remains still and central
o Face is up so that only the chin is in the water
o Eyes are looking forwards over the surface
o Shoulders should be level and square
o Hips are slightly below shoulder level
o Legs are in line with the body

Key Actions

o Push hard from the side
o Keep head up looking forward
o Stretch out as far as you can
o Keep your hands together
o Keep your feet together

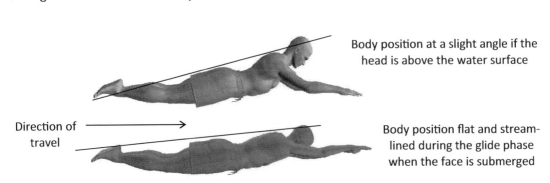

Body position at a slight angle if the head is above the water surface

Direction of travel

Body position flat and streamlined during the glide phase when the face is submerged

BREASTSTROKE: Legs

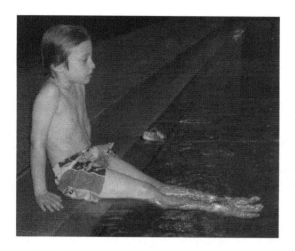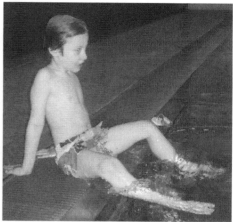

Aim: to practice the leg action whilst sat stationary on the poolside.

This exercise allows the pupil to copy the teacher who can also be sat on the poolside demonstrating the leg kick. The physical movement can be learnt before attempting the leg kick in the water.

Technical Focus
o   Kick should be simultaneous
o   Legs should be a mirror image
o   Heels are drawn towards the seat
o   The feet turn out just before the kick
o   Feet come together at the end of the kick with legs straight and toes pointed

Key Actions
o   Kick your legs simultaneously
o   Keep your knees close together
o   Kick like a frog
o   Make sure your legs are straight and together at the end of the kick

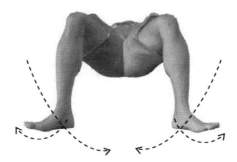

Feet turn out as the legs begin to kick round in a circular action

BREASTSTROKE: Legs

Supine position with a woggle held under the arms

Aim: to develop breaststroke leg kick in a supine position.

This allows the swimmer to see their own legs kicking. The woggle provides stability for the beginner and, with the swimmer in a supine position, allows the teacher easy communication during the exercise.

Technical Focus

o Kick should be simultaneous
o Heels are drawn towards the seat
o The feet turn out just before the kick
o Feet kick back with knees just inline with the hips
o Feet come together at the end of the kick

Key Actions

o Kick with both legs at the same time
o Keep your feet in the water
o Kick like a frog
o Kick and glide
o Point your toes at the end of the kick

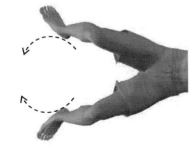

Heels drive back in a circular whip like action giving the kick power and motion

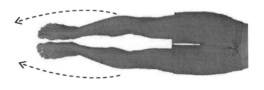

Kick finishes in a streamlined position with legs straight and toes pointed

BREASTSTROKE: Legs

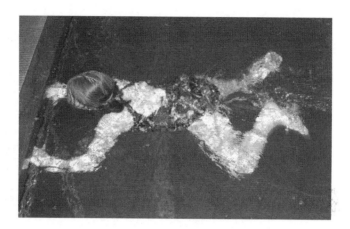

Aim: to practise breaststroke leg action in a static position.

This allows the swimmer to develop correct technique in a prone position in the water. Kicking WITHOUT force and power should be encouraged during this exercise to avoid   undue impact on the lower back.

Technical Focus

o   Legs should be a mirror image
o   Heels are drawn towards the seat
o   The feet turn out just before the kick
o   Feet kick back with knees inline with the hips
o   Feet come together at the end of the kick with legs straight and toes pointed

Key Actions

o   Kick both legs at the same time
o   Kick like a frog
o   Draw a circle with your heels
o   Make sure your legs are straight at the end of the kick

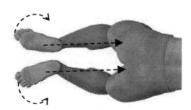

Heels drawn towards the seat and feet turn out

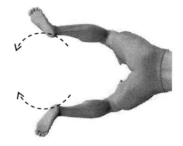

Heels draw round in a circular motion

BREASTSTROKE: Legs

Prone position with a float held under each arm

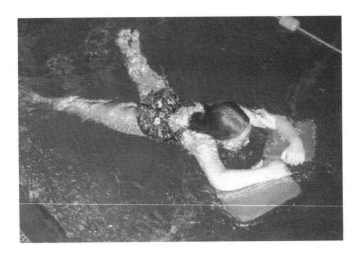

Aim: to practise and develop correct leg technique in a prone position.

Using two floats aids balance and stability and encourages correct body position whilst moving through the water.

Technical Focus
- o   Leg kick should be simultaneous
- o   Heels are drawn towards the seat
- o   The feet turn out just before the kick
- o   Feet kick back with knees inline with the hips
- o   Feet come together at the end of the kick

Key Actions
- o   Keep your knees close together
- o   Point your toes to your shins
- o   Drive the water backwards with your heels
- o   Glide with legs straight at the end of the each kick

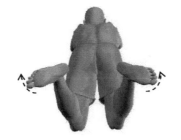
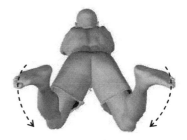

Heels are drawn up towards the seat. Soles face upwards

Feet turn outwards to allow the heels and soles to aid propulsion

Heels push back and outwards in a whip-like action

BREASTSTROKE: Legs

Holding a float out in front with both hands

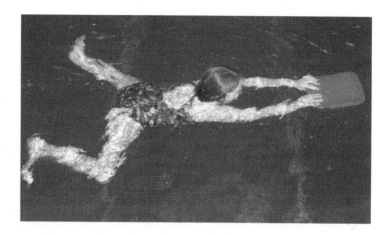

Aim: to practise and learn correct kicking technique and develop leg strength. Holding a single float or kickboard out in front isolates the legs and creates a slight resistance which demands a stronger kick with which to maintain momentum.

Technical Focus
o   Kick should be simultaneous
o   Legs drive back to provide momentum
o   Heels are drawn towards the seat
o   The feet turn out before the kick
o   Feet come together at the end of the kick with legs straight and toes pointed

Key Actions
o   Drive the water backwards with force
o   Turn your feet out and drive the water with your heels
o   Kick and glide
o   Kick like a frog
o   Make your feet like a penguin

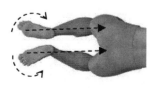

Heels drawn towards the seat and feet turn out

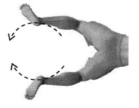

Heels drive back in a circular whip like action giving the kick power and motion

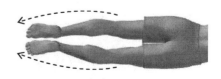

Kick finishes in a streamlined position with legs straight and toes pointed

BREASTSTROKE: Legs

Arms stretched out in front holding a float vertically

Aim: to develop leg kick strength and power.

The float held vertically adds resistance to the movement and requires the swimmer to kick with greater effort. Ideal for swimmers with a weak leg kick.

Technical Focus
o Arms should be straight and float should be held partly underwater
o Kick should be a whip like action
o Feet kick back with knees inline with the hips
o Feet come together at the end of the kick

Key Actions
o Kick your legs simultaneously
o Push the water with your heels and the soles of your feet
o Drive the water backwards with your heels

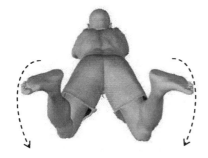

Heels push back and outwards in a whip-like action

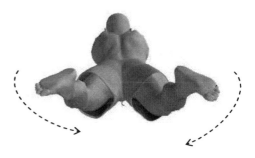

Heels drive back to add power to the kick

BREASTSTROKE: Legs

Supine position with hands held on hips

Aim: to develop leg kick strength and stamina.

This exercise is more advanced and requires the leg kick to be previously well practised.

Technical Focus

o   Kick should be simultaneous
o   Heels are drawn towards the seat
o   The feet turn out just before the kick
o   Feet kick back with knees inline with the hips
o   Feet come together at the end of the kick with legs straight and toes pointed

Key Actions

o   Keep your feet in the water
o   Kick like a frog
o   Make sure your legs are straight after each kick
o   Kick and glide
o   Point your toes at the end of the kick

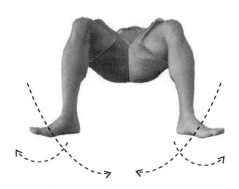

Feet turn out as the legs begin to kick round in a circular action

BREASTSTROKE: Legs

Moving practice with arms stretched out in front

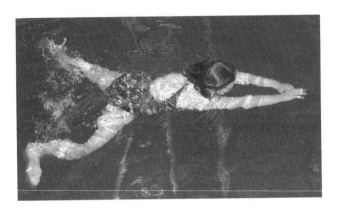

Aim: to practise correct kicking technique and develop leg strength

This is an advanced exercise as holding the arms out in front demands a stronger kick with which to maintain momentum whilst maintaining a streamlined body position.

Technical Focus
- o Kick should be simultaneous
- o The feet turn out just before the kick
- o Feet kick back with knees just inline with the hips
- o Feet come together at the end of the kick with legs straight and toes pointed

Key Actions
- o Keep your knees close together
- o Drive the water with your heels
- o Make sure your legs are straight at the end of the kick
- o Kick and glide

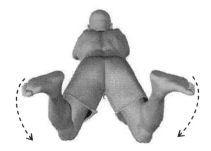

Heels push back and outwards in a whip-like action

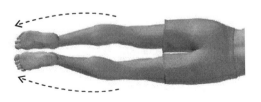

Kick finishes in a streamlined position with legs straight and toes pointed

Static practice standing on the poolside

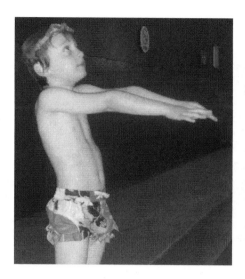 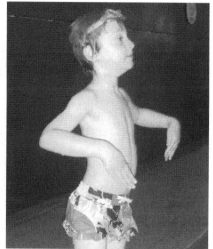

Aim: to learn the arm pull technique in its most basic form.

On the pool side, either sitting or standing, the swimmer can practise and perfect the movement without the resistance of the water.

Technical Focus
o Arm action should be simultaneous
o Fingers should be together
o Arm pull should be circular
o Elbows should be tucked in after each pull
o Arms should extend forward and together after each pull

Key Actions
o Both arms pull at the same time
o Keep your fingers closed together
o Keep your hands flat
o Tuck your elbows into your sides after each pull
o Stretch your arms forward until they are straight
o Draw an upside down heart with your hands

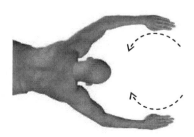 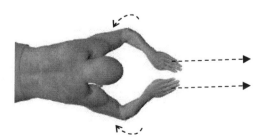

Arms and hands pull around and downwards   Elbows tuck in and arms extend forward

BREASTSTROKE: Arms

Walking practice moving through shallow water

 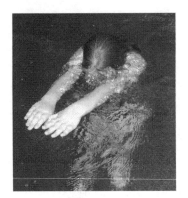

Aim: to practise and develop correct arm technique from in the water.

The swimmer can experience the feel of pulling the water whilst walking along the pool floor. Where the water is too deep, this exercise can be performed standing on the poolside. Submerging the face is optional at this stage.

Technical Focus
o   Arm action should be simultaneous
o   Arms and hands should remain under water
o   Fingers should be together
o   Arms should extend forward and together until straight after each pull

Key Actions
o   Pull with both arms at the same time
o   Keep your hands under the water
o   Tuck your elbows into your sides after each pull
o   Stretch your arms forward until they are straight
o   Draw an upside down heart with your hands

Arms and hands pull back in a circular motion

Elbows tuck in and arms and hands stretch forward into a glide

BREASTSTROKE: Arms

Moving practice with a woggle held under the arms

Aim: to learn correct arm action whilst moving through the water.

The use of the woggle means that leg kicks are not required to assist motion and this then helps develop strength in the arm pull. The woggle slightly restricts arm action but not enough to negate the benefits of this exercise.

Technical Focus

o Arm action should be simultaneous
o Arms and hands should remain under water
o Arms and hands should extend forward after the pull
o Fingers should be together
o Arm pull should be circular

Key Actions

o Pull round in a circle
o Keep your hands under the water
o Keep your fingers together and hands flat
o Pull your body through the water
o Draw an upside down heart with your hands

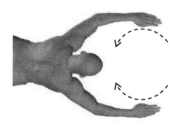
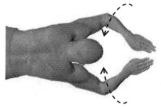

Arms and hands pull around and downwards

Elbows tuck in and arms and hands stretch forward into a glide

BREASTSTROKE: Arms

Arms only with a pull-buoy held between the legs

Aim: to develop strength in the arm pull.

The pull-buoy prevents the legs from kicking, therefore isolating the arms. As the legs are stationary, forward propulsion and a glide action is difficult and therefore the arm action is made stronger as it has to provide all the propulsion for this exercise.

Technical Focus
o Arms and hands should remain under water
o Arm pull should be circular
o Elbows should be tucked in after each pull
o Arms should extend forward and together

Key Actions
o Keep your hands under the water
o Pull your body through the water
o Keep your elbows high as you pull
o Tuck your elbows into your sides after each pull
o Stretch your arms forward until they are straight

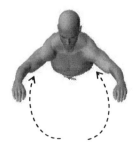

Arms and hands pull back in a circular motion

Elbows tuck in and arms and hands stretch forward together

BREASTSTROKE: Arms

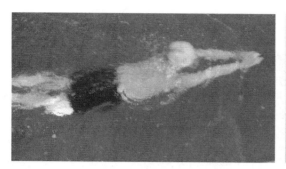 

Aim: to progress arm action and technique from previous exercises

By incorporating a push and glide, this allows the swimmer to practise maintaining a correct body position whilst using the arms. This is a more advanced exercise as the number of arms pulls and distance travelled will vary according to the strength of the swimmer.

Technical Focus

o Arms and hands should remain under water
o Elbows should be tucked in after each pull
o Arms should extend forward into a glide position
o Body position should be maintained throughout

Key Actions

o Keep your hands under the water
o Pull your body through the water
o Tuck your elbows into your sides after each pull
o Stretch your arms forward with hands together

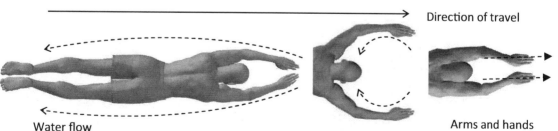

Direction of travel

Water flow

Arms and hands pull around and downwards

Arms and hands stretch forward into the original glide position

119

BREASTSTROKE: Breathing

Static practice, breathing with arm action

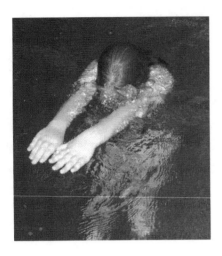 

Aim: to practise breast stroke breathing action whilst standing in the water.

This allows the swimmer to experience the feel of breathing into the water in time with the arm action, without the need to actually swim.

Technical Focus
o Breath inwards at the end of the in sweep
o Head lifts up as the arms complete the pull
o Head should clear the water
o Head returns to the water as the arms recover
o Breath out is as the hands recover forward

Key Actions
o Breathe in as you complete your arm pull
o Breathe out as your hands stretch forwards
o Blow your hands forwards

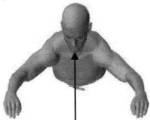

Breathe IN as the arms pull down and the head rises

Breathe OUT as the arms recover forward and the face enters the water

Breathing practice with woggle under the arms

Aim: to develop correct synchronisation of breathing and arm pull technique.

The woggle provides support which enables the exercise to be done slowly at first. It also allows the swimmer to travel during the practice. Leg action can be added if necessary. Note: the woggle can restrict complete arm action.

Technical Focus
- o Breath inwards at the end of the in-sweep
- o Head lifts up as the arms complete the pull back
- o Head should clear the water
- o Head returns to the water as the arms recover
- o Breathing out is as the hands stretch forward

Key Actions
- o Breathe in as you complete your arm pull
- o Breathe out as your hands stretch forwards
- o Blow your hands forwards

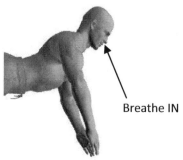

Breathe IN

Breathing in occurs as the arms pull down and the head rises above the surface

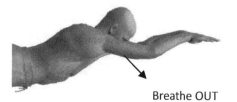

Breathe OUT

Breathing out occurs as the arms recover out in front

BREASTSTROKE: Breathing

Float held in front, breathing with leg kick

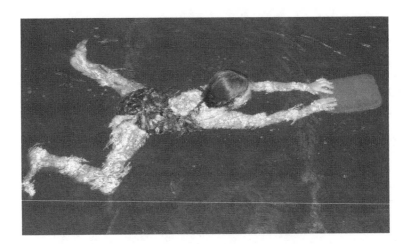

Aim: to develop the breathing technique in time with the leg kick.

The float provides stability and allows the swimmer to focus on the breathe kick glide action.

Technical Focus
- o Inward breathing should be just before the knees bend
- o Head lifts up as the knees bend ready to kick
- o Mouth should clear the water
- o Head returns to the water as the legs thrust backwards
- o Breathe out is as the legs kick into a glide

Key Actions
- o Breathe in as your legs bend ready to kick
- o Breathe out as you kick and glide
- o Kick your head down

Breathe IN just before the knees bend for the kick

Breathe OUT as the legs kick into a glide

BREASTSTROKE: Timing

Slow practice with woggle under the arms

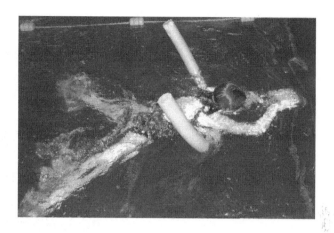

Aim: to practise the stroke timing in its most basic form.

The use of the woggle placed under the arms allows the swimmer to practice the exercise in stages as slowly as they need. It must be noted that the woggle resists against the glide and therefore the emphasis must be placed on the timing of the arms and legs. The glide can be developed using other exercises.

Technical Focus

o   From a streamlined position arms should pull first
o   Legs should kick into a glide
o   Legs should kick as the hands and arms recover
o   A glide should precede the next arm pull

Key Actions

o   Pull with your hands first
o   Kick your hands forwards
o   Kick your body into a glide
o   Pull, breathe, kick, glide

Body position starts with hands and feet together

Pull, breathe, kick, glide sequence is performed

Swimmer returns to original body position.

Push and glide, adding stroke cycles

 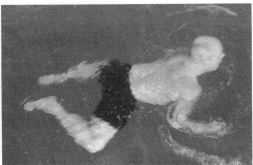

Aim: to practise and develop correct stroke timing.

The swimmer starts with a push and glide to establish a streamlined glide. The arm pull, breath in and then leg kick is executed in the correct sequence, resulting in another streamlined glide.

Technical Focus

o From a streamlined position arms should pull first
o Legs should kick into a glide
o Legs should kick as the hands and arms recover
o A glide should precede the next arm pull

Key Actions

o Kick your hands forwards
o Kick your body into a glide
o Pull, breathe, kick, glide

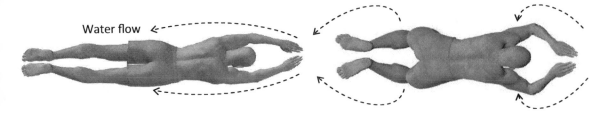

Water flow

Push and glide to establish body position

Pull, breathe, kick and glide again

BREASTSTROKE: Timing

Two kicks, one arm pull

Aim: to perfect timing whilst maintaining a streamlined body position.

From a push and glide, the swimmer performs a 'pull, breathe, kick, glide' stroke cycle into another streamlined glide. They then perform an additional kick whilst keeping the hands and arms stretched out in front. This encourages concentration on timing and coordination and at the same time develops leg kick strength.

Technical Focus
o Legs should kick into a glide
o Legs should kick as the hands and arms recover
o A glide should follow each leg kick
o Head lifts to breath with each arm pull

Key Actions
o Kick your body into a glide
o Pull, breathe, kick, glide

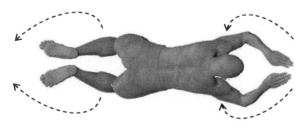

A full stroke cycle is performed from a push and glide

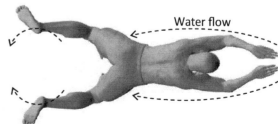

Additional kick whilst the hands and arms remain still

BREASTSTROKE

Aim: to swim full stroke Breast Stroke demonstrating efficient arm and leg action, with regular breathing and correct timing.

Technical Focus
o Head remains still and central
o Shoulders remain level
o Leg kick is simultaneous
o Feet turn out and drive backwards
o Arm action should be circular and simultaneous
o Breathing is regular with each stroke cycle

Key Actions
o Kick and glide
o Kick your hands forwards
o Drive your feet backward through the water
o Keep your fingers together and under the water
o Pull in a small circle then stretch forward
o Breath with each stroke

| Heels draw up towards the seat and feet turn out | Arms pull in a circular action and elbows tuck in | Legs kick backwards providing power and propulsion | Arms stretch forward into a glide |

Breaststroke

Exercise quick reference guide

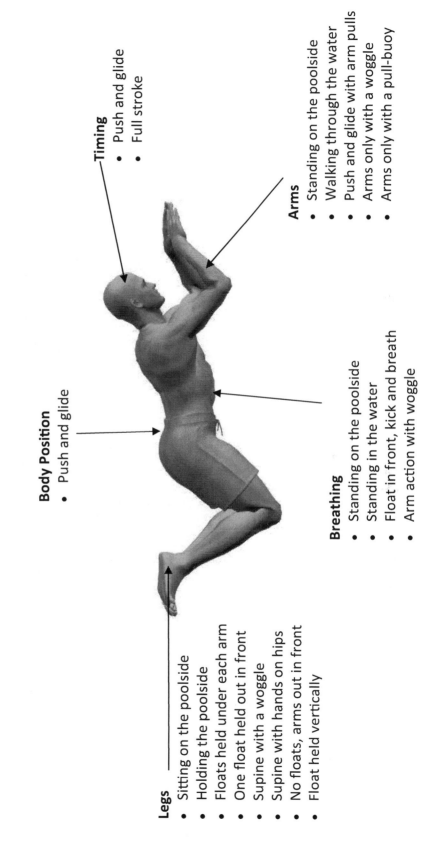

Timing
- Push and glide
- Full stroke

Arms
- Standing on the poolside
- Walking through the water
- Push and glide with arm pulls
- Arms only with a woggle
- Arms only with a pull-buoy

Body Position
- Push and glide

Breathing
- Standing on the poolside
- Standing in the water
- Float in front, kick and breath
- Arm action with woggle

Legs
- Sitting on the poolside
- Holding the poolside
- Floats held under each arm
- One float held out in front
- Supine with a woggle
- Supine with hands on hips
- No floats, arms out in front
- Float held vertically

butterfly

stroke exercises

BUTTERFLY: Body Position

Aim: to practise the body position and movement by holding on to the poolside.

The swimmer performs an undulating action whilst using the poolside or rail for support.. Note: this exercise should be performed slowly and without force or power as the static nature places pressure on the lower back.

Technical Focus
o Exercise should be slow and gradual
o Head remains central
o Shoulders and hips should be level
o Horizontal body with an undulating movement
o Wave like movement from head to toe
o Legs remain together

Key Actions
o Keep your head in the middle
o Make the top of your head lead first
o Keep your shoulders level
o Keep your hips level
o Make your body into a long wave

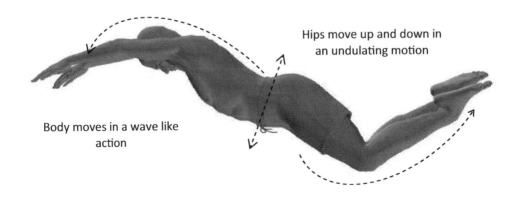

Hips move up and down in an undulating motion

Body moves in a wave like action

130

BUTTERFLY: Body Position

Dolphin dives

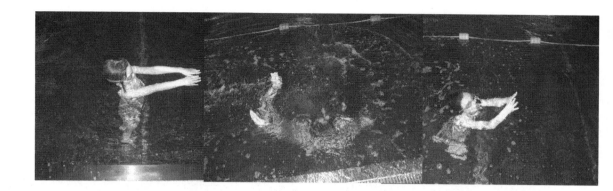

Aim: to develop an undulating body movement whilst travelling through water of standing depth.

The swimmer performs a series of dives from a standing position, diving deep under the surface, arching the back and resurfacing immediately to stand up. The aim is to perform as many dolphin dives across the width as possible. Swimmers can then progress to performing the practice without standing in-between dives.

Technical Focus
o Head remains central
o Shoulders and hips should be level
o Body moves with an undulating movement
o Wave-like movement from head to toe
o Legs remain together

Key Actions
o Keep your head in the middle
o Make the top of your head dive down first
o Make your body into a huge wave
o Stretch up to the surface

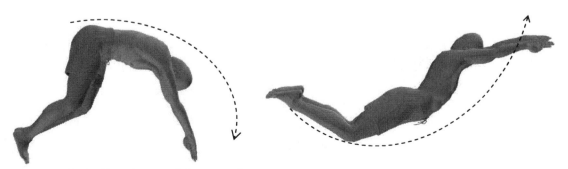

Body dives down and then resurfaces immediately in a wave like movement

131

BUTTERFLY: Body Position

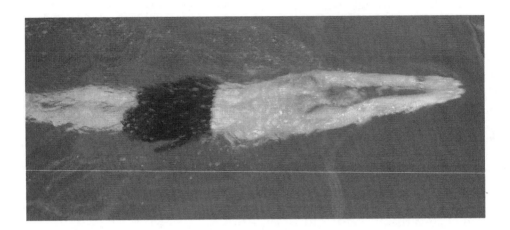

Aim: to practise and develop an undulating whilst moving.

The swimmer pushes from the poolside into a glide and then begins the undulating action from head to toe. This allows the swimmer to experience the required undulating action whilst moving through the water.

Technical Focus
o Head remains central
o Shoulders and hips should be level
o Body is horizontal with an undulating movement
o Wave-like movement from head to toe
o Legs remain together

Key Actions
o Make the top of your head lead first
o Keep your shoulders level
o Keep your hips level
o Make your body into a long wave
o Pretend you are a dolphin swimming

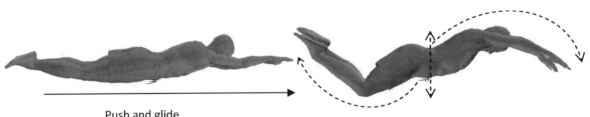

Push and glide

Body moves in a wave like action

BUTTERFLY: Legs

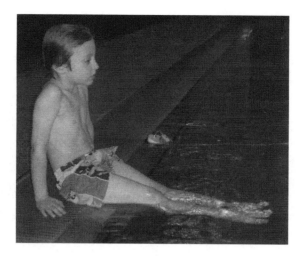

Aim: to develop the kicking action whilst sitting on the poolside.

Bending and kicking from the knees with legs together allows the swimmer to practise the correct movement and feel the water at the same time.

Technical Focus
o Simultaneous legs action
o Knees bend and kick in upbeat to provide propulsion
o Legs accelerate on upbeat
o Toes are pointed

Key Actions
o Kick both legs at the same time
o Keep your ankles loose
o Keep your legs together
o Point your toes

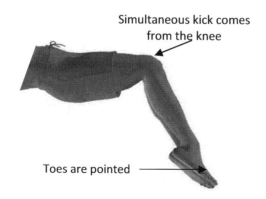

Simultaneous kick comes from the knee

Toes are pointed

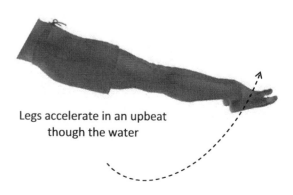

Legs accelerate in an upbeat though the water

133

BUTTERFLY: Legs

Push and glide adding leg kick

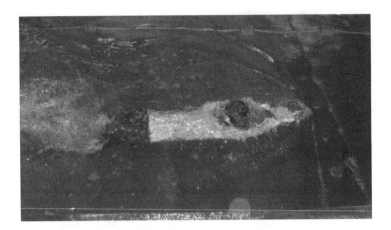

Aim: to practise the dolphin leg kick action and experience movement.

This allows the swimmer the develop propulsion from the accelerating leg kick and undulating body movement.

Technical Focus
o Simultaneous legs action
o Knees bend and kick in downbeat to provide propulsion
o Legs accelerate on downbeat
o Toes are pointed
o Hips initiate undulating movement

Key Actions
o Keep your ankles loose
o Kick downwards powerfully
o Keep your legs together
o Point your toes
o Kick like a mermaid

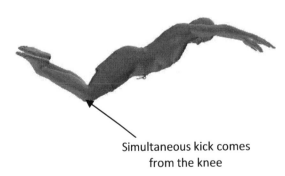

Simultaneous kick comes from the knee

Legs accelerate in an downbeat to provide propulsion

BUTTERFLY: Legs

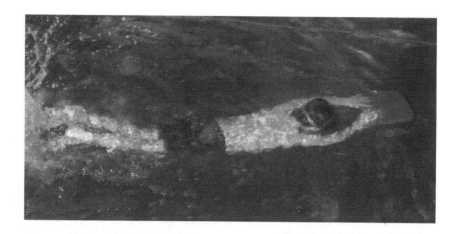

Aim: to develop the leg kick using a float for support.

This practice allows the advanced swimmer to develop leg kick strength and stamina as the float isolates the legs.

Technical Focus
o Simultaneous legs action
o Knees bend and kick in downbeat to provide propulsion
o Legs accelerate on downbeat
o Toes are pointed
o Hips initiate undulating movement

Key Actions
o Kick with both legs at the same time
o Kick downwards powerfully
o Keep your legs together
o Create a wave-like action through your body
o Kick like a mermaid

Powerful leg kick provides propulsion and help the body to undulate

Supine position with arms by sides

Aim: to practise and develop a dolphin leg kick in a supine position.

This allows the swimmer to kick continuously whilst facing upwards. This practice requires a great deal of leg strength and stamina and therefore is ideal for developing these aspects of the stroke.

Technical Focus
o Simultaneous legs action
o Knees bend and kick in upbeat to provide propulsion
o Legs accelerate on upbeat
o Toes are pointed
o Hips initiate undulating movement

Key Actions
o Kick both legs at the same time
o Keep your ankles loose
o Kick upwards powerfully
o Keep your legs together
o Point your toes

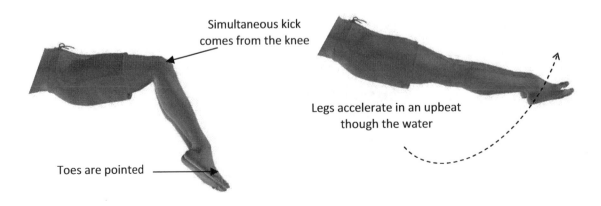

Simultaneous kick comes from the knee

Legs accelerate in an upbeat though the water

Toes are pointed

Aim: to combine the leg kick and undulating body movement and perform a rolling motion through the water.

This practice can be performed with arms held by the sides or held out in front. The rolling motion forces the swimmer to use the head, shoulders and hips to produce the movement required for powerful undulating propulsion.

Technical Focus

o Simultaneous legs action
o Head and shoulders initiate rolling motion
o Knees bend and kick to provide propulsion
o Legs accelerate on downbeat
o Hips initiate undulating movement

Key Actions

o Kick both legs at the same time
o Keep your ankles loose
o Roll like a cork screw
o Keep your legs together
o Make your body snake through the water

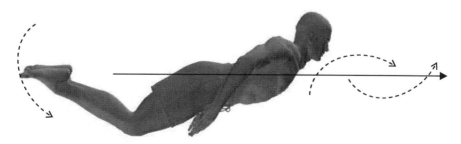

Legs kick and body performs a 'cork screw' like roll through the water

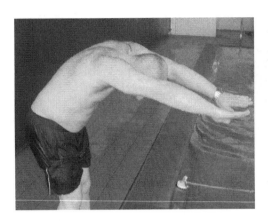 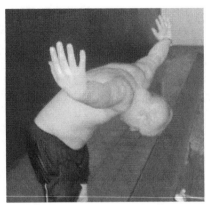

Aim: to practise correct butterfly arm action whilst standing on the poolside.

The pupil is able to work through the arm action slowly and in stages so as to experience the basic movement required.

Technical Focus
o Arms move simultaneously
o Hands enter the water in line with the shoulders
o Hands pull in the shape of a keyhole
o Hands push past the thigh

Key Actions
o Move both arms at the same time
o Thumbs go in first
o Draw a keyhole under your body
o Push past your thighs

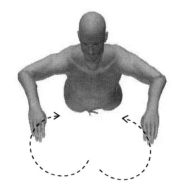 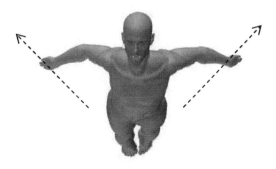

Arms pull through in a keyhole shape

Arms pull through and past the thighs

BUTTERFLY: Arms

Aim: to progress from the previous practice and develop the arm action.
The swimmer can get a feel for the water whilst walking and performing the simultaneous arm action.

Technical Focus
o Arms move simultaneously
o Hands enter the water in line with the shoulders
o Hands pull in the shape of a keyhole
o Hands push past the thigh

Key Actions
o Move both arms at the same time
o Thumbs go in first
o Draw a keyhole under your body
o Push past your thighs

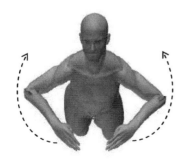

Arms pull through simultaneously

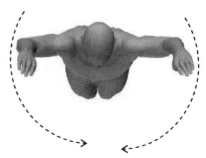

Arms are thrown forwards over the water surface

BUTTERFLY: Arms

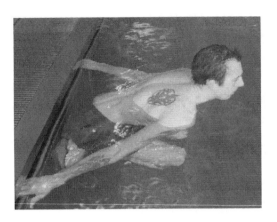 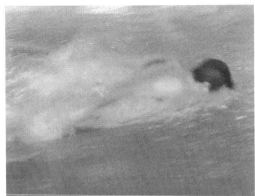

Aim: to practise the arm action whilst moving through the water.

Correct body position is established from the push and glide and the swimmer can then use the arm action to maintain momentum through the water. A limited number of arm pulls can be achieved with this practice.

Technical Focus
o Arms move simultaneously
o Fingers closed together
o Thumbs enter the water first
o Hands enter the water in line with the shoulders
o Hands push past the thigh
o Hands clear water surface on recovery

Key Actions
o Move both arms at the same time
o Thumbs enter water first
o Pull hard through the water
o Pull past your thighs
o Throw your arms over the water

Arms pull through and push past
the thighs

Arms recover over the water surface

BUTTERFLY: Arms

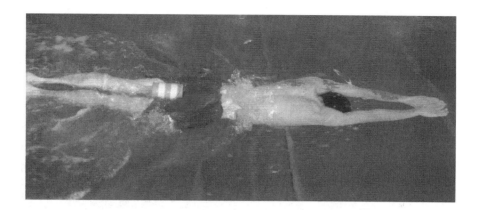

Aim: to help the swimmer develop arm strength and stamina.

This practice is performed over a longer distance, progressing from the previous practice. The pull buoy provides buoyancy and support as well as help the undulating body movement.

Technical Focus
o Arms move simultaneously
o Fingers closed together
o Thumbs enter the water first
o Hands enter the water in line with the shoulders
o Hands push past the thigh
o Hands clear water surface on recovery

Key Actions
o Thumbs go in first
o Pull hard through the water
o Pull past your thighs
o Throw your arms over the water

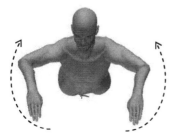

Arms pull through the water with power

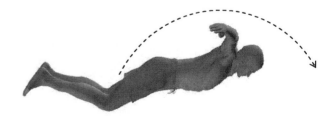

Hands and arms clear the water on recovery

BUTTERFLY: Arms

Arm action with breaststroke leg kicks

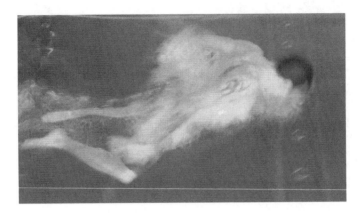

Aim: to enable use of breaststroke leg kicks to support the arm action.
As the legs kick, the propulsion helps the body to rise and the arms to recover over the water surface. This practice is also a good introduction to the timing of butterfly arms and legs.

Technical Focus
o Thumbs enter the water first
o Hands pull in the shape of a keyhole
o Hands push past the thigh
o Little finger exits the water first
o Hands clear water surface on recovery

Key Actions
o Thumbs go in first
o Draw a keyhole under your body
o Pull past your thighs
o Little finger comes out first
o Throw your arms over the water

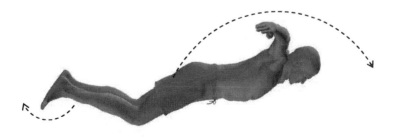

Leg kick help the arms to recover over the water surface

BUTTERFLY: Breathing

Aim: to incorporate butterfly breathing into the arm action.

This practice is performed standing either on the poolside or stationary in water of standing depth.

Technical Focus
- Breathing in should occur as the arms sweep up and out
- Explosive breathing is most beneficial
- Chin should remain in the water
- Face dives into the water as the arms come level with the shoulders
- Breath can be taken every stroke cycle or alternate cycles

Key Actions
- Blow out hard as your chin rises
- Put your face down as your arms recover
- Push your chin forward and breathe every arm pull or every two arm pulls

Breathing occurs as the arms sweep up and out

Face submerges at the arms recover

Aim: to use the full stroke to practice breathing, incorporating regular breaths into the arm and leg actions.

Technical Focus
o Breathing in occurs as the arms sweep upwards
o Breathing in occurs as the legs are kicking downwards
o Explosive breathing is most beneficial
o Chin remains in the water
o Face dives into the water as the arms come level with the shoulders
o Breath can be taken every stroke cycle or alternate cycles

Key Actions
o Blow out hard as your chin rises
o Lift your head to breathe in as your legs kick down
o Put your face down as your arms come over
o Push your chin forward and breathe every arm pull or every two arm pulls

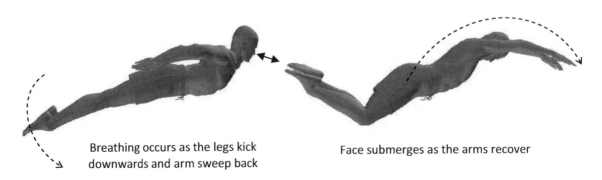

Breathing occurs as the legs kick downwards and arm sweep back

Face submerges as the arms recover

Aim: to perform the full stroke butterfly, incorporating two leg kicks per arm pull.

Technical Focus

o Two legs kicks per arm cycle
o Legs kick once as hands enter and sweep out
o Legs kick once as arms sweep up and out

Key Actions

o Kick hard as your hands enter the water
o Kick again as your hands pull under your body

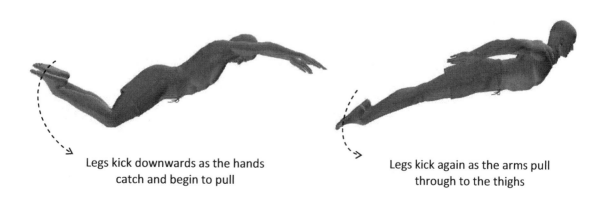

Legs kick downwards as the hands catch and begin to pull

Legs kick again as the arms pull through to the thighs

Butterfly

Exercise quick reference guide

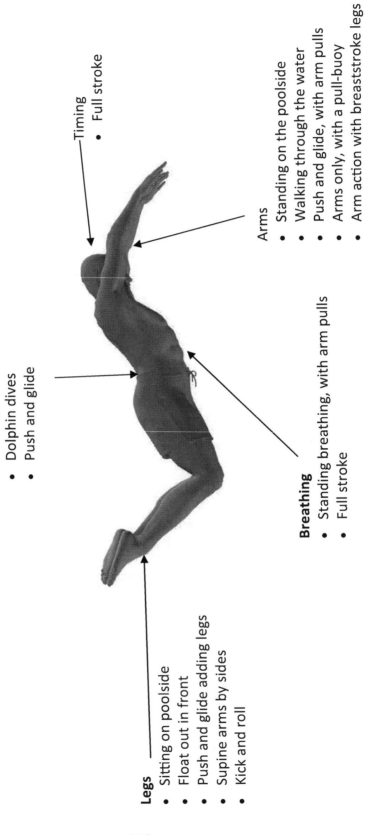

Body Position
- Holding pool rail
- Dolphin dives
- Push and glide

Timing
- Full stroke

Arms
- Standing on the poolside
- Walking through the water
- Push and glide, with arm pulls
- Arms only, with a pull-buoy
- Arm action with breaststroke legs

Breathing
- Standing breathing, with arm pulls
- Full stroke

Legs
- Sitting on poolside
- Float out in front
- Push and glide adding legs
- Supine arms by sides
- Kick and roll

index

stroke exercises

Front Crawl   Page

Backstroke

Page

Body Position

Legs

Arms

Breathing

Timing

Full Stroke

Quick Reference

Breaststroke Page

Butterfly   Page

FOL
FEB 1 5 2024

Made in the USA
Lexington, KY
11 March 2018